DEV
DEMONOLOGY
IN THE 21ST CENTURY

KATIE BOYD

Schiffer
Publishing Ltd

4880 LOWER VALLEY ROAD, ATGLEN, PENNSYLVANIA 19310

Ouija is a registered trademark of Parker Brother's Games

Schiffer Books are available at special discounts for bulk purchases for sales promotions or premiums. Special editions, including personalized covers, corporate imprints, and excerpts can be created in large quantities for special needs. For more information contact the publisher:

Schiffer Publishing Ltd.
4880 Lower Valley Road
Atglen, PA 19310
Phone: (610) 593-1777;
Fax: (610) 593-2002
E-mail: Info@schifferbooks.com

Please visit our web site catalog at **www.schifferbooks.com**

We are always looking for people to write books on new and related subjects. If you have an idea for a book, please contact us at the above address.

This book may be purchased from the publisher. Include $5.00 for shipping. Please try your bookstore first. You may write for a free catalog.

In Europe, Schiffer books are distributed by:
Bushwood Books
6 Marksbury Ave.
Kew Gardens
Surrey TW9 4JF
England
Phone: 44 (0)208 392-8585
Fax: 44 (0)208 392-9876
E-mail: Info@bushwoodbooks.co.uk

Website: **www.bushwoodbooks.co.uk**
Free postage in the UK. Europe: air mail at cost.
Try your bookstore first.

Designed by Stephanie Daugherty
Type set in Trajan Pro/NewBskvll BT/Goudy Initialen

ISBN: 978-0-7643-3195-4
Printed in the United States of America

DEDICATION

or my Mother, Barbara, and for Beckah, thank you for always showing me the light in those times when all I saw was darkness.

ACKNOWLEDGMENTS

hanks to Dinah Roseberry, my editor, for allowing me free reign during the writing of this book. Thanks to all who work at Schiffer Publishing; you're all great; and to Ghost Quest crew members, Beckah (Tolley) Boyd and Raven Duclos, for all your support during the writing process. Thanks to Denise McMahon, of Bridge to Natural Wellness, for adjusting my back when I sat for too many hours writing. Thanks to everyone who sent me those wonderful e-mails containing encouragement and interest in my Demonology and Occult work.

CONTENTS

AUTHOR'S NOTE

am an experienced, and highly trained Demonologist and Occult Sciences Expert. You will find, within this book, true accounts of spirit hauntings, demonic hauntings, possession, and occult rituals. Names have been changed to protect the identity and privacy of each person. This book also contains symbols, legends, and in some instances, partial rituals, simply for the purpose of general and historic interest. I do not condone nor endorse any inexperienced person to attempt to summon or manifest any entity contained mentioned here.

This book is not a course in Demonology, and does not give all the knowledge needed to perform exorcism, or banishment of negative or demonic entities. Inexperienced groups, or people trying this out for themselves, please do your research, or better yet get a professional demonologist to come with you on hunts for your own safety. Remember, you never know what you're going into, and what may seem very quiet, may indeed harbor something far more darker.

INTRODUCTION

 y name is Katie Boyd; I am a Demonologist/Exorcist/ Occult Sciences Expert from the New Hampshire area and I am writing this book as a resource for those of you out there looking to get into the field of demonology and the paranormal. Mind you, this is a starting-off point; you won't learn everything you need to know in this book. However, it will give you an awesome start. I love to learn new techniques and views in the paranormal but have been unable to find a comprehensive resource book for demonology or exorcism. So I decided to write one, in hopes that it would reach you and others with similar interests. My mission is to help you get a jump start on an education into a world we still know barely anything about, except through mythology.

Demonology, exorcism and the occult has gained a lot of attention recently with new paranormal television and radio shows out each day. They are all seeking the answers to the unexplained, asking for knocks and bangs from spirits. Spirits—that's the big thing right now; unfortunately, there aren't many groups out there with a good knowledge about demons, at least none on the television. Though, it's not uncommon to see a movie or watch a show, which contains some form of demon or demonic issue—typically in a fantasy or cartoon setting. We make fun of what we fear to make ourselves feel safe, and in doing so, we are crippling our society. The belief in demons has diminished, but that's okay, they want it that way.

We have always been taught one basic truth: where there is good, there is bad, for every good day you have, inevitably, there will be a bad day. It is called polarity, however, most of us aren't cognizant of this phenomena spiritually. Most of us can recognize evil when we see it, whether human or otherwise; it is built into our DNA, this sensitivity to danger. It's our mechanism for survival, hence why when we sense someone is a "danger," for instance, and then cross the street when they come in our path. Demonic entities and homes that are haunted trigger this same mechanism, it is a feeling of fear, and a driving need to hide or leave. However, there are a few of us out there who ignore this instinct and have learned how to overcome the danger of that which can't be seen.

Occultism and Demonology is not something I picked, but in fact was called to. Since I have answered that calling, it and all things paranormal have become my passion. I started very young and remember when I used to read books behind my mother's couch all about the occult; they would talk about conjuring spirits. I read the works of John Dee, King Solomon, and other famous twelfth-, thirteenth- and fifteenth-century occultists and magicians. As I got older, I became obsessed with learning; I found out these "spirits" or "angels" that were being summoned by these Master Occultists were actually demons, and that those who summoned them would pay for the favors of the demons with their lives, or other things precious to them such as power or family. I have met others with similar interests and through the years have realized that although the texts that taught me about demons were ancient, they still existed and thrive in our society's disbelief.

Prior to joining Ghost Quest (a paranormal research group), I worked on my own, gathering knowledge and helping those that I could. When, by chance (I like to call that fate), I walked into the store the ghost group was operating their headquarters out of at the time, and saw how open they were to my way of working, it was a blessing. I became a co-founder of the team and it has given me the ability to help so many more than I had when I'd worked alone. It has also brought to light within my community the fact that occultism is not evil or negative, but a neutral tool that can be utilized if handled properly. We as a team have taken on demons and negative spirits from all different spiritualities, from Catholic to Buddhism traditions.

This book is part memoir, part guide, part case file; in it you will discover the world of the demonic in our society today, you will learn everything you need to know about the hierarchies, possession, exorcism, negative entities, evil entities in different cultures, and what it is like to be a twenty-first century demonologist and occultist. But my main reason for writing this narrative is not to entertain, but to empower you because education is power and ignorance isn't bliss—what you can see in this world can hurt you, but what you can't can kill you. Be prepared.

PART I
DEMONOLOGY

Hans Memling Paintings, Musee des Beaux Arts, Strasburg.

DIARY OF A TWENTY-FIRST CENTURY DEMONOLOGIST

any think a Demonologist's primary resources are folklore and legend. Although that is partially true, we also keep an eye on patterns in today's society, such as areas of high paranormal activity and tracking instances of demonic possession. There are many different ways to do this: networking with other paranormal groups and tracking instances of extreme violence and activity through newspapers are the best tools, but that is the tip of the iceberg. I have over nineteen years experience and training in demonology and I must admit that dealing with these entities is never boring. Many people would like to think that demons are headed toward extinction, because people are believing in them less and less. It is easy to believe in a loving and all-powerful God, but harder to imagine a dark, drooling demon. However, demons are not a dying breed; in fact they surface daily, in people, in things, and in places. They are not monsters under the bed, but real incorporeal living energy with the ability to create chaos, wreak havoc, and destroy.

Being a demonologist is not a common occupation—it is not mainstream. When asked what I do for a living, I cannot simply state I am an accountant and then have everyone understand my work. When I say, "I am a demonologist and an occultist with over nineteen years experience in both theses fields," most give me odd looks and then proceed to grill me about my work and experience. Others, however, will simply walk away in disbelief. People always love to read stories of horror, but that is fiction—we know it isn't real. When I am recounting a story of a demonic haunting, most are eager to hear it, but they do not necessarily believe it, mostly out of fear. Demonic entities do not feed off fear, although that does allow an easier way to keep a person down. It is better to believe and be prepared than to make fun of or refuse to believe. Be open to the concept.

Being a demonologist is kind of like working in a prison: you are surround by negative people and entities almost twenty-four-seven; it can wear you down if you let it. But it is the most fulfilling work I have ever found, because for a family dealing with a demonic entity, I can be almost like a torch for them, ridding the home or person of the darkness and pain surrounding them. I don't do my work for the money; it's not about getting famous or rich. It's about helping, and when I have done my job and a family or person is finally able to move on with their lives in a positive way, that is all the payment I need.

Throughout this book, we will discuss what it is like to be a demonologist and to be called on to a case, as well as the process I have to go through before performing any type of exorcism. Within that spectrum of the field there are still a lot of holes and pitfalls. You must take everything into account about the person or family's environment, state of mind, and physical health. We will touch on all aspects of this field, and hopefully, answer any questions you may have.

When I'm called in to investigate a case, I have to first evaluate the individual's state of mind and medical background—such as medications an individual might be on, if an individual is in counseling, or seeing a medical doctor for depression or any forms of paranoid delusions. If my findings with an individual are medical and not demonic or spirit related, I always refer them to a medical professional who will help them. Then I determine what "kind" of spirit is causing the activity within the client's home or business. I'll write down all the information a client can recall on the strange activity, and then I will narrow it down as to which form of "spirit" or "demonic" is causing these problems.

Some demonologists will collect evidence and pass it along to church authorities. My methods are a lot different and I do not report to anyone other then myself and the Ghost Quest members who are participating in the case. I learned the art of banishing demonic entities at a very young age through the study of twelfth-, thirteenth- and fourteenth-century occultism. I have learned the necessary words, signs, seals, and sigils to summon, banish, and exorcise a demonic entity from a person, place, or object. Yes, those who use the traditional methods of exorcism have challenged me and my techniques and style of exorcism, but I have found my method more efficient and safer for both the possessed individual and myself.

During many of my investigations, it seems that negative spirits were behind a lot of the paranormal activity, one out of one hundred cases actually have some form of demonic activity going on. I never leave home without my exorcism kit. This metal box contains relics, seals, holy waters, and incantations—enough to banish high-level demons or evil spirits of every religion. I have come across so many holy men and women who believe that the words and rituals of their Deity is enough to cast out demonic entities. I agree and disagree. The holy words of different faiths do work, but usually only long enough for the family to escape, and pray that they aren't followed. The words and seals before many of today's mainstream religions seem to work just as well, if not better, than many of the modern techniques used for exorcism.

A lot of times before I decide to take on or investigate a demonic case, the entity will try to scare me away, sometimes by attacking loved ones. For example once, after getting a call from a woman who was demonically haunted, I was out at a convenience store to pick up half and half for my coffee. My spouse, who is a psychic medium, called me, calmly explained that there was a small black mass on the ceiling in our kitchen. We knew it wasn't a spirit, or a negative thoughtform and came to the conclusion that is was a warning. It was not the first time we had seen something like this. My spouse began saying prayers out loud, and casting it out. When I arrived home, my spouse was still in the process of this and together we banished the demonic messenger. It is not an uncommon occurrence to be warned sometimes. I am not the first demonologist who will tell you that—many others who have broken into the mainstream have talked about phenomena occurring in the home prior to a banishment, exorcism, or investigation. I have heard a dog-like growling, had horrible visions while sleeping, smelled foul odors, or our phone will ring during certain times and only static will be heard on the other end. Dark figures will slip by me or I'll catch a glimpse of one out of the corner of my eye. These are only a few warning signs I've been given to back off a case. The more serious a haunting, the more serious the signs can be.

Demonic entities can smell danger more then a mile away, and that's never good. Why? That makes it hard to plan a sneak attack, but knowing Occult knowledge gives me an advantage over any higher or lower demonic entity. Demons are intelligent and clever; remember they have been around a lot longer then you and I. But we do have an advantage in that, for as long as humans have been around, we have been studying them, and thanks to the written and spoken word, we still have many of the old beliefs and diehard "cures" for this spiritual ailment.

Since I have been working in and around the demonic scene for over nineteen years, I have studied and experienced a lot, and one of the inhuman spirit's favorite games is "mind messing." One day, my spouse and I were talking about a supposedly demonically-infested abandoned town. We thought that it might be cool to investigate with our paranormal group. After the conversation, I continued on with my agenda for the day. Later that night, I was attacked by a vision of my mother standing inside a decrepit wood boardroom. There was an old bed she stood next to, and the smell indicated extreme rot of both the house and every living thing in it. I knew it was located in part of the town I was speaking about earlier that day. My mother was not alone. I could see the room clearly and everything inside the room, including small demonic entities crawling on the walls. Did I mention that my mother had passed three years ago? This was not my mother—I recognized right away the handy work of demonic entities. I had always felt guilt for not being able to say good-bye to my mother before she had passed and they knew that—tried to use it against me to break me down.

One thing is for sure, demonic entities don't play fair, for she was standing before me with feeding tubes hanging from her mouth and white fluid coming out of the tubes. I was not scared, but was furious! And you never infuriate a demonologist—especially me! So I played their game right back and wrapped my hands around my mother's neck (again this was a vision not a real person), rather around that demonic entity's neck claiming to be my mother, and popped its head right off. The vision ended rather quickly when they realized that this method was not working on me. Only a selected few individuals knew about my mother's passing and how it affected me, but demonic entities know far more about us then we could ever imagine.

Being a co-founder and a co-owner of the paranormal research group, Ghost Quest, not only am I dealing with demonic entities, but also negative or evil spirits. What I need to make clear is this: Negative spirits can also give a person warning signs to stay away from a case. Once, two members had their computers crash right after loading pictures of an investigation; one was mine. Also, one might experience terrible headaches while traveling to a client's home or business, or even symptoms of feeling sick and nauseous. The negative spirit is saying, *turn around now or else*.

Much like anything else, there are levels of evil. Most people confuse evil or negative spirits with demonic entities, as their trademarks are very similar. However, spirits are entities that have lived and died, demons have never lived as a human, animal or plant. Negative spirits are usually people who have crossed violently, were violent in life, and some just want attention—either way, once passed, their spirit never crossed over and they continue to cause pain and anguish, either for revenge or as a reenactment of their time when living. Demons are more powerful then any negative spirit could ever be, they have their own energy source to create manifestations, where as spirits oftentimes must draw from an outside source to manifest even a tenth of what an inhuman entity can.

Some cases that I have investigated, I was finding demonic entities with negative spirits working for them. Again, this is an often occurrence because the negative spirits are weaker than the demonic and easily mastered by a more powerful energy. In those cases, when I am not with the paranormal research group I belong to, I will have my spouse, who like I have mentioned is a psychic medium, deal with clearing the negative spirits while I take care of the demonic entities.

It is imperative that the demonic entities be removed first, so they cannot interfere with the psychic's work. If this is not done, then the medium can become open to attack when he or she is in a state of trance or psychic opening.

Speaking on the subject of psychics, I want to clear up one issue that I have come across while lecturing, investigating, or just surfing the Internet. I have listened and read all about the reasons why psychics should not be involved in a negative spirit or demonic case. That's a load of crap. Psychics can be a very valuable asset when working with a demonologist. I am often on the Internet or with my nose in a book keeping up on the latest news, tracking activity, and learning the newest techniques. I have come across a few web sites that state, "Bringing a psychic into a negative environment will heighten the amount of phenomena because their abilities empower the spirit or demonic entities." I personally have never experienced a psychic creating more of a disturbance within one of my investigations. It would be like any person trying to make spirit contact—either things would happen or they wouldn't. In fact, any medium worth their salt would have at one time or another come up against negative spirits. Most psychics have learned to setup a protection when entering a demonic or negative home. They will also have learned how to clear or banish negative spirits. So I personally believe that unless the psychic is completely new to the game, they should do just fine and not up the level of activity during an investigation or exorcism. If they are just learning to access and use their abilities, then yes, I will agree that it would be an unstable situation as the psychic may not know how to protect themselves against attack from negative spirits or entities. But I do not know where the varied sources get their information regarding this. It is unfortunate and sad to see mediums degraded in such a way when they are so valuable to the demonology and paranormal profession. I never leave home without one!

In the field, I have come across many, many types of people. Occasionally there are a few with mental disorders, who believe they are possessed or have demonic entities in their home. There is actually a little-known mental disorder called "Demonomania" or "Demonopathy" which means the individual believes he or she is possessed by demons, not usually a singular entity, but many. Most of the claims are hard to investigate, as true reality and personal perception of that reality are very blended. Although some of the claimed phenomena may be part of mental illness or a warped perception of reality, there are those occasions when there is something else entirely going on. Sometimes there is nothing, yet no matter what the demonologist may say, it will not matter. The mentally ill individual will still insist that demons are running around their home and/or trying to make that person go crazy.

But we can speak more on the subject of mental illness and demonic activity later.

I've noticed through the media or just surfing the Internet, that more and more individuals are claiming to be demonologists and occult specialists. I am thrilled that there is such an interest in these fields. However, I have found that although most have an interest in the title, they do not have the commitment to train or feel the need for study. This makes them susceptible to not only put themselves in danger, but their colleagues and friends as well. Demonic entities know what you know, and if they realize you have no actual knowledge about them and no experience with them, well, your in BIG trouble! If you would like to become a demonologist or occult specialist, you should seek a teacher with more than ten years experience in either field. Do not go in blind.

I have also found many people willing to teach the craft of demonology or the occult whose practices are unfounded and untested. In other words, they really don't know squat. Research your possible teacher before agreeing to train with them; it is of incredible importance that whichever field you choose to undertake, you are well trained, because both are dangerous and you could potentially bring harm, not just to yourself, but to friends and family. Trust me; no one ever just wakes up one morning and wants to become a demonologist. My childhood experiences determined the road in which I was meant to travel.

GROWING UP HAUNTED

I grew up in Goffstown, New Hampshire on a hill a short distance from center of town. My house was a beautiful white two story with a big back yard. On the outside, this house looked like a typical suburban home, however, an evil hid within the house.

For the first time in my life, I am sharing my story of the haunting terror that my family and I went through. In the year 1971, my parents moved my brother and I to the town, Goffstown. Through the first few years, my father and grandfather renovated most of our house. We had a huge living room off our den area which my father made into a hairdressing shop for my mother. All new wallpaper was placed on the walls of every room, new dark wood kitchen cabinets and storage cabinets were placed in the kitchen, new carpets were put in and all new electricity was installed throughout the house. My father was always working on some innovative project to improve our home.

Our basement was beneath our kitchen and the basement door was located in the kitchen. There was also a staircase which led to three bedrooms and a bathroom upstairs—creepy place to be alone at night; I would never, even as a teenager, stay upstairs alone at night.

My first memory of a terrifying paranormal experience was around six years old. I was upstairs playing with my brother (who is about three years older then I) in his room. We were playing with some Hot Wheel™ cars by my brother's bed on the floor. For some odd reason, I turned and looked into the bedroom doorway, which was located across the room. Standing there was a large burnt figure with broad shoulders, not moving at all. There was no face, no eyes or hair, no features at all. I was blinded by fear and suddenly started running and screaming out of my brother's room and ran down the hall and into my mother who was worried by the screams.

Not soon after my experience in the bedroom, every night at 12:00 am, I would wake up from a nightmare and run very fast into my parents' room. These nightmares always showed me skulls and skeletons in a large wooden box. Now, my parents never let my brother or I watch scary movies or read scary books, so something else was lurking within my nightmares. When I was around seven years old and still having nightmares every night, while sleeping, I was dreaming of a bunch of trees, and skeletons running all around trying to tie me to one of those trees. Meanwhile, outside my house, a windy storm was brewing; wind was blowing and the rain was coming down heavy. Suddenly, I started screaming at the top of my lungs and something would not let me get out of bed. My father came running into my room and just as he reached for me, a huge *bang* hit the roof of my room. After I was safe in my parents' room, my father found out that a huge tree had just fallen on our roof. Sure could be just coincidence...or maybe not.

Over the years, so much happened while living in that house. Lights in certain rooms would turn on when off. My name would be called out in my father's voice, only when I was home alone. Objects would disappear and be either found somewhere in the house or never found again—such as my mothers rosary beads, which went missing and no matter where we all looked, the rosary beads just couldn't be found. There was always a sense of being watched, didn't matter what area of the house a person would be in. The basement was even creepier. Every time I would go down in the basement, something was there with me. I would see out of the corner of my eye something moving fast in the shadows. Right away, the sense of not being wanted anywhere in the basement was very obvious. No matter how many times myself or any member of my family would turn off the basement light, it would turn right back on.

As more years passed living in the house, more and more disagreements would break out. My parents suddenly were fighting, my father and brother started fighting, my brother and I started fighting, even our dog and cat weren't getting along. Something needed to be done.

I was in my early teens when my mother had our local priest come and do a blessing on our house. It seemed to work for awhile, but the activity came back full force. Rage seemed to fill my household and my family turned against each other—it was awful to see a loving family fall apart. My father became very silent and my mother seemed to loose her mind a little; it was crazy. At 2:00 am in the morning my mother would come into my room screaming at me to re-clean the house which we had done that afternoon. My brother became violent with me, yelling in my face and hitting me. And as for myself, I became withdrawn and kept to myself most of the time.

All the paranormal activity still went on, but when I turned sixteen, my parents divorced and my brother, soon after, moved out and on his own. At the age of eighteen, I too moved out. Now it was just my mother living in the house. After five years had passed, my mother's health was not going good and she decided to sell the house and move out of state to be with my brother. A few years passed and so did my mother, bless her soul.

While writing this book and doing some research on the town, I came across a lot of history. During 1810, the population in the town was around 2,000 people; they had all settled in the quaint village. You may ask what on earth did they do to taint the soil—and this is just what they did. There are many who believe that parts of Goffstown (possibly including the center) were built on unmarked graves. Secret societies were prominent within the town around the late 1800s, such as Knights of Pythias 1890s, Granite Lodge 1887, Independent Order of Good Templars 1869, Mystery Rebekah Lodge 1891 and more. Native blood was spilled upon the soil of Goffstown when the town was built. There were strange happenings including fires starting on their own that were burning the villagers' homes, a high murder rate, and many suicides (Goffstown High School is still known by some to be called, "Suicide High.").

In the early 1970s, Goffstown's local priest drove out a group of Satanic worshipers dwelling in the woods. This is just some of the town's history—scary huh? Years and years later, I took a trip back to Goffstown and saw my old house way up on that hill. As I pulled over on the side of the road, I sat in my truck for a while—yeah, the evil is still there inside that house.

HISTORY AND EXISTENCE

arth and its religions are based on polarities, night and day, man and woman, good and evil. Demons have been around since we realized this, although many of today's evil entities started out as pagan gods. Such as Ba'al who was originally a grain god to the Phoenicians. The word demon is actually from the Greek "Daimon" which means "intelligent." In our society of science and "reality," we have become relaxed in the subject of evil. When we think of evil, we picture rapists, murderers, and muggers—not demons that are out to steal one's soul. To really understand evil, we need to know its root.

Ancient cultures, such as the Babylonians and Assyrians, believed evil spirits and demons were everywhere; these entities would travel only at night and gain entrance into the home through cracks or holes. During the day, their homes were mountain tops, shadows, graves—anywhere isolated. Demon's were referred to as Alu, Utukku were spirits, and Gallu was Devil. They were blamed for everything from headaches to murder. In Sumerian texts, they talk about three different categories or classes of demons, the first and most common being spirits who couldn't find rest, the second being half demon-half human entities, and the third being full demonic which were on the same level of divinity as a god but a polar opposite. Assyrians, Babylonians, and Sumerians all had similar negative entities in common, such as the Alu and Utukku, but Sumerians also had other entities such as Labartu, the daughter of Anu, with the head of a lion; she was known to eat both animals and humans whole, especially enjoying their blood.

As you can see, even within the Babylonian and Assyrian cultures, they believed that anything negative that happened was evil. When we were still a primitive people, and to this day in some cultures, it was believed that anyone with mental illness was inhabited by an evil entity. Back then, there were no psychologists, no sciences, no prescriptions, except for herbal cures. Anything that could not be cured or understood was evil. These poor souls would either be exorcised, banished, or shunned, the community believing that the sick person would taint the village or its harvest. Exorcism was actually the preferred method dispelling evil because if one survived he or she could stay within the community. Although the person would still be considered an outcast, at least they wouldn't starve or freeze to death. Again, that is if they survived; exorcism could take between two months to a couple of years, and was extremely dangerous. It

Gustav Dore's "Fallen Angels" from John Milton's Paradise Lost c. 1866.

included fasting, constant prayer and beatings, with the idea that by making the body uncomfortable, the demon would not want to continue to inhabit it—in short, it was torture.

Why don't we move forward a couple of centuries to the most recognized mainstream authority on demons and demonology, the Bible. In the Gospel of Mark, Jesus casts out many demons from those afflicted with ailments and illnesses. We can assume from this statement that the thought of evil and sickness has not changed, so what, we must ask ourselves, has caused some to believe that demons are actually real and not just illness? Well, some hold to the belief that these entities are in fact fallen angels and He cast them into an abyss called Hell that was to be like a prison. The punishment would not be physical, rather, the angels would be deprived of the sight of God for eternity, which is for them the worst punishment. However, it is believed that Earth was middle ground, both good and evil could inhabit this plane. It is thought that because they held such hatred for God (because He cast them out), they began to rebel and destroy what He had created, meaning us—sickness is believed to be one of the tools in their arsenal. Tempting and inducing us to sin is another big gun aimed at our heads. It is believed that the first attempt was made when one of these angels came as a serpent to trick Eve into picking the forbidden fruit. She shared this fruit with Adam; when their eyes were opened to good and evil, they were cast from paradise.

Who can talk of demons without speaking of the Prince himself, Lucifer (which translates from Latin to "the Light-Bearer"); he is also known as the Adversary. This entity started the war with God when he believed he could lead heaven; his pride was his downfall.

In the thirteenth century, the Bishop of Tusculum, John XXI, estimated that along with Lucifer, 133,306,668 angels were cast out over a total of nine days. The Bishop was a highly educated and philosophical man whose favorite subjects were theology, metaphysics, and logic. He died on May 20, 1277, eight days after a room in his house collapsed on him. Supposedly, he was writing a heretical text at the time of the accident.

Alphonso de Spina was believed to be a partial author of a text called the Fortalitium Fidei, typically referred to as the Fortalitium. This treatise was divided into five separate books, showing the mentality at the time by Catholicism towards people of other religions. The first four books were mainly about "converting" non-believers such as the Jewish and Muslim population. However, the fifth and last book was dedicated to battling the Devil, and included detailed information regarding the banishment of the entities, their hatred of humans, what abilities they have, etc. He also reaffirmed what the Bishop of Tusculum claimed regarding the actual amount of fallen angels. However, there is no information regarding how either person came to that particular number.

Let us journey back to the Son of God, the most well-know exorcist, demonologist and priest in history; while he was on earth, he cast millions of demons from villages, homes, and people. It was evident the power He held over them. You can clearly see this in Mark 5:1 -18, the story of the demon possessed man:

"When he saw Jesus from a distance, he ran and fell on his knees in front of him.

He shouted at the top of his voice, "What do you want with me, Jesus, Son of the Most High God? Swear to God that you won't torture me!"

For Jesus had said to him, "Come out of this man, you evil spirit!"

Then Jesus asked him, "What is your name?"

"My name is Legion," he replied, "for we are many."

And he begged Jesus again and again not to send them out of the area.

A large herd of pigs was feeding on the nearby hillside.

The demons begged Jesus, "Send us among the pigs; allow us to go into them."

He gave them permission, and the evil spirits came out and went into the pigs. The herd, about two thousand in number, rushed down the steep bank into the lake and were drowned."

He was able to free these victims by commanding and casting out the entities, binding them and forbidding their return. Jesus also gave this knowledge to some of his trusted disciples, who continued on his mission to free the world of evil, and bring healing to the sick after his death. Buddha also had these abilities, as did the Egyptian Horus, and numerous sun gods in different religions throughout time have shown these same characteristics. Polarities are still a big part of mainstream religion, with good, must come evil.

THE CATHOLIC DEMONS

n this chapter, we will take a look at the demonic entities within the Catholic and Christian belief system. *Why do they have their own chapter?* you may ask. Well, because they have heck of a lot of entities. These entities are also the most popularized form of inhuman spirits, both in the media and in the religion itself. How many times have you seen depictions of angels versus demons on your television or in your local movie theater. It doesn't go away, and that's okay; the media desensitizes us to their presence and that is exactly how they want it. The list I have created is in complete alphabetical order. Within the biography of the entity, you will come to realize some of their weaknesses, forms, and where they are mentioned in the Bible. You will also hear some interesting things, such as a particular demon can be summoned to give you all knowledge. Tempting isn't it? But alas, there is always a price, and usually a contract, it seems that Catholic demons prefer to have a written agreement. They seem to personify the business world in the demonic realm. There have been many victims who have "sold their soul to the devil" usually for a selfish purpose—a typical reason is money, then power, and fame. Ultimately, they died before they were truly able to have their wishes fulfilled.

Rarely do the demon's within the Court appear on earth, but rule from their thrones in hell, although sometimes, they will send minions from the lower ranks to fulfill their bidding. Typically, a lower demon that is looking to scare a demonologist or exorcist will use a higher demon's name instead of their own. "I am legion for we are many," is not just a famous line in the Bible, but a truth when it comes to lower demonic entities, for most of their names were never told or were lost through time, and there are many

ABADDON

It is said that when the last days fall upon earth, Abaddon shall be given a key to open the abyss and unleash demons free to roam on earth. In the Old Testament, this demon's name is mentioned over five times and is also known as "The Destroyer" and "King of the locusts" in The Book Of Revelations. If a individual dares to summon this demon, it shall show itself as a large human locust.

ABIGOR

This demon is in command of sixty legions of lower demons. Unlike most demons, Abigor usually shows himself as handsome.

AGARES

Having a power which can stop any form of motion, Agares can force people in hiding or on the run to turn around and go back. This demon also has the power to cause earthquakes. When Agares is summoned, the demon is seen as a decrepit old man who has a hawk on one of its fists and rules thirty-one legions of lower demons.

AGUARES

Known to be a master linguist, which possess humans through dancing, Aguares commands thirty-legions of lower demons.

AIM

Aim portrays itself as a handsome gentleman with three heads, one of a man, one of a cat, and the last of a serpent. This demon is known to set fires to cities and other large areas, and if called upon, Aim will give true answers to all questions of a personal nature which you were either afraid to ask or didn't want anyone to know about. Aim rules over twenty-six legions of other lower demons.

ALLOCER

If this demon is summoned, one will be taught all the mysteries of the sky. Allocer commands thirty-six legions of demons and will sometimes appear looking like a man with a horned lion's head. Tends to ride a horse with dragon legs.

AMAYMON

Be careful of this demon for its breath is very poisonous But if one has a silver ring which is charged in the proper way and worn on the middle finger, then this demon cannot harm an individual with its breath.

AMDUSCIAS

Commands twenty nine-legions. Known for making disturbing music. This demon's true form is said to be that of a unicorn, but comes in human form when summoned. Legend says that trees will bend at his command.

AMON

Handles all marching orders of forty-legions. This is a demon that can vomit flames and has a wolf head with a tail of a serpent, some also say this demon looks like a man with a ravens head and dog like teeth. If a individual makes a "pact" with Satan, they will be given knowledge by Amon. Also known as Aamon, this demon has the gift of prophecy and can make predictions of the future.

ANDRAS

Works a lot with the demon Flauros and is highly dangerous, if one tries to summon. Andras will try to lure the summoner out of their magic circle and give instant death if protection is not taken. This is a very unpleasant demon to work with and tends to use a individual's anger against one's self.

APOLLYON

This demon is mentioned in "The Book Of Revelation" (9:7-11) as the one who leads the locust plague at the end of days.

"And the shapes of the locusts were like unto horses prepared unto battle; and on their heads were as it were crowns like gold, and their faces were as the faces of men. ⁸ And they had hair as the hair of women, and their teeth were as the teeth of lions. ⁹ And they had breastplates, as it were breastplates of iron; and the sound of their wings was as the sound of chariots of many horses running to battle. ¹⁰ And they had tails like unto scorpions, and there were stingers in their tails: and their power was to hurt men five months. ¹¹ And they had a king over them, which is the angel of the bottomless pit, whose name in the Hebrew tongue is Abaddon, but in the Greek tongue hath his name Apollyon".

This is the great dragon of chapter 12, Satan or Azazel. He has a number of names, but in each case, he is the king of all the demons, Lucifer, who became Satan."

(Revelation 9:11)

Christian and Apollyon.

CHRISTIAN'S COMBAT WITH APOLLYON

The Pilgrim's Progress From This World to That Which is to Come by John Bunyan. Illustrations by H.C. Selous and M. Paolo Priolo, London, Carsell, Petter and Galpin c. 1850.

ASMODEUS

Known to be invoked by King Solomon during the first century to aid in the construction of his temple. Since the last 3,000 years, Asmodeus has been recorded throughout history, such as in the "Book of Tobit." This is a powerful demon of lust and is personally responsible for stirring up marital problems. Also commands twenty-two legions of lower demons. A powerful element against this demon is water, for Asmodeus despises it.

ASTRAROTH

This demon is known for having regrets about the rebellion against God in Heaven and considers itself to be innocent. Here is and excerpt from The Goetia about this demon.

"He is a Mighty, Strong Duke, and appeared in the Form of an hurtful Angel riding on an Infernal Beast like a Dragon, and carrying in his right hand a Viper. Thou must in no wise let him approach too near unto thee, lest he do thee damage by his Noisome Breath. Wherefore the Magician must hold the Magical Ring near his face, and that will defend him. He gives true answers of things Past, Present, and to Come, and can discover all Secrets. He will declare wittingly how the Spirits fell, if desired, and the reason of his own fall. He can make men wonderfully knowing in all Liberal Sciences. He rules forty Legions of Spirits."

BALAM

This demon is one who always gives the individual correct and perfect answers to any question. If summoned, Balam will grant the gift of being invisible. Remember to ask for the formula to change back from being invisible; demons will never remind the individual. Commands over forty legions of lower demons.

BATHIN

This is a female demon who has all knowledge of stones and herbs. If one dares and summons Bathin, she has the power to instantly bring a individual from one country to another. She commands thirty legions of demons and will come to a summoner looking like a strong woman with a serpent tail and rides upon a pale-looking horse.

BEEZLEBUB

When Lucifer first started his rebellion against heaven, he recruited several very powerful angels such as Beelzebub. He is known as "Lord of Things That Fly" and also " Lord of the Flies." Beelzebub traits are causing destruction though tyrants, causing demons to be worshiped among people, and to bring priests to lust. In the Old Testament, Beelzebub was the Philistine god of Ekron. Also, during the Salem Witch trials Beelzebub's name was mentioned repeatedly. Beezlebub was also more than once summoned by King Solomon who had by the gift of God been given power over all demonic entities. Here is a conversation that had been recorded between them:

"And again I summoned Beelzebul, the prince of demons, to stand before me; and I sat him down on a high seat of honor and asked him: "Why are you alone, prince of demons?"

He told me: "Because of (all) of heaven's angels descended, I alone am left. For in the first heaven, I was first angel, named Be'el-zebul ["Lord of heaven"].

And now I control all those who are bound in Tartarus..."

I, Solomon, asked him: "Beelzebul, what is your job?"

He replied to me: "I destroy kings. I ally myself with tyrants. And I send my own demons, so that men may believe in them and be lost. And I incite God's chosen servants, priests and pious men, to want wicked sins, evil heresies and lawless deeds. And they obey me and I carry them to destruction. And I inspire men with envy and murder, wars and sodomy, and other evils. And I will destroy the world..."

I said to him: "Tell me, by what angel are you checked?"

He replied: By the holy and precious Name of God Almighty, whom the Hebrews call by a string of numbers totaling 664; and with the Greeks it is "Emmanuel"; and when a Roman orders me by the great name of the power of Eleeth, I vanish immediately."

I, Solomon, was amazed when I heard this. And I commanded him to saw up Theban marbles. And when he started sawing the marbles, the other demons shrieked out loud, howling for their king."

~*Pseudepigrapha*, Testament of Solomon 6:1-4, 8-9 [ms. P]

BELETH

Also known as Bilet, Bileth and Byleth. Now, if one even dares to summon this demon, please be careful. The summoner must be very brave and no matter what the demon may look like, stand your ground. Hold a hazel wand and in the air towards South and East direction and make a triangle, this demon will be trapped within this triangle for only a short time. Beleth commands eighty-five legions of lower demons. An excerpt from the Goetia about Beleth:

"The Thirteenth Spirit is called Beleth (or Bileth, or Bilet). He is a mighty King and terrible. He rideth on a pale horse with trumpets and other kinds of musical instruments playing before him. He is very furious at his first appearance, that is, while the Exorcist layeth his courage"

~ *S.L. MacGregor Mathers (1904)*

BELIAL

One, of Satan's most respected demons and was one of the first fallen angels to be expelled from Heaven. Within the Dead Sea scrolls, Belial was the original leader of the forces of evil. Until the New Testament firmly established Satan as the "leader of the dark side." Balial was also named the unofficial demon of lies. In some older texts and scripts this demon is also known as Matanbuchus, Mechembuchus, and Meterbuchus.

BELPHEGOR

This demon likes to seduce humans to inventions that will make them rich, with always a price to pay. If an individual tries to summon this demon, it will be rather difficult, for most do not know the secrets. But if one does succeed, there is a "pact" to make with this demon which is always collected sooner then later. Sometimes Belphegor is seen as a naked woman who is beautiful or a bearded demon who is hideous to see.

BERITH

This demon is terrible and very powerful. Commands twenty-six legions and tells the truth when asked about the past, present and future. Also can turn metals into gold. This demon shows itself only wearing red clothes and has a golden crown upon its head. Here is a quote from the Lesser Keys Of Solomon which I thought might be interesting.

"Le tresor d'Albert Petit" (XIII), a method of conjuring him under a form resembling can be found. On a Monday night a black chicken is bled at a crossroads. One must say: 'Berith will do all my work for twenty years and I shall recompense him.' Or else one may write the spell on a piece of virgin parchment with the chicken's blood. The demon thus evoked will appear the same day, and put himself completely at the conjuror's disposal. But after twenty years, Berith will claim his reward for services rendered."

BIFRONS

If this demon is summoned, one will gain knowledge of the arts, gems, woods, and herbs. Has the power to move a corpse from one place to another place. Sometimes Bifrons will move corpses from one place to another place and even make those graves glow. This demon will always show itself as a monster and only commands six legions of lower demons.

BOTIS

If one is looking to know secrets of the past or future, this is the right demon to ask. Botis, if summoned, will bring past friends and future friends together, also will bring enemies together. This demon commands sixty legions of lower demons and can be seen as a large viper or a human with large teeth and two horns.

BUNE

This is a powerful and strong demon who commands thirty legions of lower demons. If summoned, one will be given true answers and riches if Bune is feeling the mood of giving. Bune can change the human dead into demons, and then command them to do his biddings.

CAACRINOLAAS

Commands thirty-six legions of lower demons and inspires murder among humans. Where Caacrinolaas inspires murder, it is also known to create a love between enemies. This demon appears as a dog with griffin wings. Johann Weyer wrote *Pseudomanarchia Daemonum* in 1577 and speaks of Caacrinolaas:

"Glasya Labolas, alias Caacrinolaas, or Caassimolar, is a great president, who commeth forth like a dog, and hath wings like a griffen, he giveth the knowledge of arts, and is the captaine of all mansleiers: he understandeth things present and to come, he gaineth the minds and love of friends and foes, he maketh a man go invisible, and hath the rule of six and thirtie legions."

CAIM

This demon commands thirty legions of lower demons. If one dares to summon Caim, the individual will know all answers about the future and be given all knowledge to understand the voice of birds and other animals. Watch out for this demon; when summoned, comes in the form of a man standing on hot coals.

CORSON

This is highly dangerous demon who commands seventy-two legions of lower demons. If one does dare to summon Corson, it needs to be on a Holiday, otherwise will follow.

CROCELL

When this demon is summoned, it will appear as a dark angel and will speak in a mysterious and dark way. Crocell will teach the summoner all areas of the liberal sciences. Has a talent to heat all bodies of water. Also commands forty-eight legions of lower demons.

DANTALION

A dangerous demon to summon for Dantalion can reveal an individual's deepest and darkest secret, can give hallucinations, and transport an individual to any part of the world. When summoned, this demon will appear in many different ways and always is holding a mysterious book in its hands. Is seen sometimes as a man and sometimes as a woman.

ELIGOS

This demon when summoned will show an individual the secret to all hidden discoveries and knows all future outcomes of wars. When summoned, Eligos will be seen as a good knight carrying a lance and upon a horse. This is no ordinary horse, for the demon Beezlebub made a horse for Eligos out of the remains of a horse from "The Garden Of Eden." Commands sixty legions of lower demons.

EURYNOME

Not to be confused with the Greek Titan of the same name, Eurynome is most often seen as a half man-half dog type creature with huge predatory teeth, and wearing animal skins to cover sores that are all over its body. This demon is often depicted sitting upon vultures' skin and Pausanias once said he fed upon dead flesh and carrion. One can see a statue of this demon in the temple of Delphi. Eurynome is considered to be a very aggressive and brutal demon of death.

FOCALOR

Commands thirty-three legions of lesser demons and is seen in the form of a man with griffin wings. After 1,000 years, Focalor had hoped to be able to return to heaven, but it seems this demon was deceived. It has great power over the wind and oceans. Also has the power to drown both men and women.

FLAUROS

If this demon is summoned into a magic triangle, it will speak of information about all other fallen angels. It also speaks true answers to all questions about the past, present and the future. Flauros will appear like a leopard or like a strong man figure with flaming eyes. This is a dangerous demon who uses fire to destroy its enemies, especially exorcists.

FORCAS

This demon is also known as Furcas and Forras, it typically appears as an old hermit-like man with long white beard and hair, riding a horse, and carrying a pointed dart. He teaches logic to all lower demons and the wonders of herbs and precious stones. Forcas commands the 290 legions of demonic forces. He is able to make people invisible, to enhance speaking abilities, and is known to restore lost items.

FURFUR

Watch out if an individual summons this demon; one needs to command Furfur into a magical triangle. For then all answers asked by the conjurer will be truthful. Also Furfur commands twenty-nine legions of lower demons.

GREMORY

This demon does not command, but over sees twenty-six legions of lower demons. When summoned, one will be told about all hidden treasures and will be granted love of any woman. Gremory is seen as a beautiful woman riding a camel.

GUSION

Commands forty legions of lower demons and is seen when summoned as a baboon. When this demon is asked any question by a summoner, they will be shown the real meaning behind the question. Gusion has the power to bring together all lost friends and family.

LEONARD

Sometimes also called "Le Grand Negre" which means The Black Man. In folklore it is suggested that Leonard has a goat's body from the waist up with three large horns upon his head with two fox ears and eyes that reflect Hell's fire. There are reports which state that this demon may also appear as a bloodhound or a black bird. During the black witches Sabbaths, it is said this demon will appear.

LERAJE

Also known as Loray or Oray, this entity commands thirty legions of lower demons. Often depicted as a beautiful man carrying a bow and set of arrows, all dressed in green. This is a dangerous demon that can cause great battles and arguments. Watch out because this demon is also know to infect wounds caused by arrows.

LEVIATHAN

A great angel, which fell from heaven with Lucifer, transformed into a demon bound to the sea. He waits in the water to devour the souls of the damned on Judgment Day. Leviathan is commonly known as The Prince of Liars and much like a slippery eel he can avoid exorcism by even the most highly trained and experienced of demonologists. It is said his powers, and ability to swallow mass amounts of souls is feared by both God and men.

LUCIFER

Throughout the Christian history, Lucifer was known as the mightiest archangel in heaven. He became self-centered and motivated by pride to lead a revolution against God. When Lucifer's rebellion failed, he was caste out of heaven along with a third of the heavenly host. These fallen angles came to reside in our world and are still here today. At some point in time, while Lucifer fell from heaven, his name changed to Satan. And all the angels that followed to earth, became known as demons. Satan is concerted to be the most embodiment of evil and God's worst enemy.

> *"How art thou fallen from heaven*
> *O day-star, son of the morning! (Helel ben Shahar) How art thou cast down to the ground, That didst cast lots over the nations!*
> *And thou saidst in thy heart:*
> *I will ascend into heaven, Above the stars of God (El) Will I exalt my throne;*
> *And I will sit upon the mount of meeting, In the uttermost parts of the north; I will ascend above the heights of the clouds; I will be like the Most High (Elyon).'*
> *Yet thou shalt be brought down to the nether-world, To the uttermost parts of the pit."*

~ Isaiah 14:12-15

LUCIFUGE ROFOCALE
Lucifuge only takes form of a human body at night; he dislikes lights and can kill by breath or touch. This demon has many jobs such as, the infection of disease and deformity, creation of earthquakes, and the destruction of many sacred deities.

MALPHAS
A dangerous demon who will try and deceive the summoner even if given a gracious sacrifice. Malphas will appear as a crow, but only by request and while in a human form shall talk in a rough-like animal voice. This mighty demon can destroy all buildings built by enemies and will share all thoughts by the enemy, but only per request of the summoner.

MARCHOSIAS
A powerful demon who commands thirty legions of lower demons. This demon is great fighter and very strong, so be careful if one wishes to summon Marchosias. If summoned, all questions shall be answered in truth. After 1,200 years,

Marchoias thought that it would be possible to return to heaven with all the non-fallen angels, but it never happened.

MORAX

If Morax is summoned, this demon looks like a large bull with a face of a man. Also will teach all areas of Astronomy and shall give the summoner wise and faithful familiars. These familiars give all knowledge of herbs and stones. Commands a legion of thirty-six demons.

MURMUR

Murmur is not just any demon, but a demon which can summon the souls of the dead and let the conjurer ask any question. If this demon is summoned forth, two lower demons will appear and make the sound of trumpets. Some conjurers claim that Murmur is seen as a soldier riding a vulture. Commands thirty legions of lower demons.

NABERIUS

A demon who commands nineteen legions of lower demons and if summoned shall appear as a bird with three heads. Naberius will restore honor and dignity to those who feel they have lost it and makes those who summon him wise in the ways of science, art and rhetoric.

OROBAS

Commands twenty legions of lower demons. This demon if summoned will only give true and factual answers to questions of the past, present and future. Also will give true answers to the real creation of the world. Orobas is a faithful demon for anyone who has the courage to summon and is seen as a horse, but will change into a man upon request.

OSE

Commands only three legions of lower demons. If one summons this demon, only true answers will be given and all secret knowledge shall be known. Ose will bring insanity to anyone the conjurer wishes and suddenly an individual will believe they are a monster or creature.

PAIMON

This demon is the most obedient to Lucifer than any other demon. Commands 200 legions of lower demons. Paimon if summoned, will answer all questions, but the conjurer must answer questions in return. Paimon will teach the conjurer all the secrets about philosophy and science and will reveal all mysteries of the earth, wind, and water.

PHENEX

If a conjurer is not alone when calling upon this demon, make sure all other individuals block their ears. If not, one shall become deaf by the singing voice of Phenex. Commands twenty legions of lower demons and will teach a conjurer all areas of sciences and poetry. As many other of these demons, Phenex hopes that after 1,200 years, heaven will welcome this demon back.

PRUFAS

It is said that this demon is made out of flames and sometimes can be seen outside "The Tower of Babel." Prufas, if summoned, will only cause one to quarrel and bring falsehood and has a habit of lying to the summoner. Commands twenty-six legions of lower demons.

PURSON

Only in human form will this demon share all secrets of the divine and all secrets of the creation of our world. If summoned, listen, for one will be able to hear trumpets before Purson arrives. Commands twenty-two legions of lower demons.

RONOVE

A taker of old souls and often comes around to harvest souls of injured or very sick humans. Also takes souls of animals which are near death. If summoned, one will learn the art of rhetoric, languages, and be given loyal servants to help in all magical areas. Commands twenty legions of lower demons.

SABNOCK

This is a rather nasty demon, who will cause wounds on humans and make them suffer for days. After several days have passed, then this demon will make the wounds become infected and then fills those wounds with worms. Commands fifty legions of lower demons.

SARGANTAS

This demon loves to sneak into a human's mind and shares its own inner most thoughts in that mind. If one tries to summons this demon, watch out for those intense hallucinations.

SEERE

Is in control of 261 legions of lower demons. Seere will travel to the ends of the earth in seconds to do all bidding of the conjurer's wishes. If summoned, one might see a beautiful man riding upon a winged horse.

SHAX

A dangerous demon to try to summon, and if one does try, it must be called into a magical triangle. Shax will follow all wishes of the conjurer and take away the sight and hearing, and steal any object the conjurer wishes. Never ask this demon for familiars, for they will always deceive and lie. Commands thirty legions of lower demons.

STOLAS

Commands twenty-six legions of lower demons. Be careful with this demon, for is a collector of innocent souls. Stolas will send lower demons out to torture and capture all the souls of boys and girls. If summoned, one will gain all knowledge of astronomy and knowledge of all poisonous plants.

SURGAT

This is a lower demon and does not command any legions. Sugat is one of the very few lower demon names that is recorded through history, such as in "The Grimoire of Pope Honorius the Third." Also if summoned, it will open any lock for that individual.

VALAC

This is not a physically harmful demon. If summoned, one will learn where all serpents are hiding in the world and will be given true answers to all questions. Commands thirty-eight legions of lower demons and sometimes can be seen as a small poor boy with angel wings.

VALEFAR

A commander of ten legions of lower demons. This demon seems to tempt individuals to steal and brings friendships among thieves. But, Valefar will always deceive and bring death to anyone who summons it.

VEPAR

Commands twenty-nine legions of lower demons. A very dangerous demon, for Vepar controls water and makes the sea or any body of water rough and stormy. Also, this demon makes humans die in three days by putrefying wounds and letting worms breed inside wound. Only a conjurer can stop this demon by commands and then all wounds will quickly heal.

VINE

Commands thirty-six legions of lower demons. Vine if summoned, can make all witches known and can bring on storms for the summoner. Is seen as a lion holding a snake in the left paw.

VORDELET

It is said that this demon makes sure all black witches get to the Sabbaths safely and on time.

VUAL

Commands thirty-seven legions of lower demons and speaks in a Egyptian type language. If summoned, will grant love of a woman and grants friendships of anyone the conjurer wishes. Always will give true answers to all questions of past, present and future.

XAPHAN

During the time of the angels rebellion in heaven, Xaphan suggested he would set heaven on fire. This demon is one of the original demons to have fallen from heaven and down to our world.

ZAGAN

Commands thirty-three legions of lower demons and has a power to turn all metals into gold. Will make men and women smart and witty, will turn a fool into a wise individual. Zagan also has the power to turn blood into wine, and wine into blood.

ZEPAR

Commands twenty-two legions of lower demons and can be seen as a soldier in red clothes wearing armor if summoned. Loves to seduce women, and if asked, will change form into their beloved. If a women deceives this demon, one will soon become sterile.

AUTHOR'S NOTE

Most often I am called upon to banish such demons or demonic entities which inexperienced individuals summon. I do not recommend summoning such demons as listed above for any reason. I wrote only what happens if these demons are summoned, according to old occult texts and personal knowledge; I do not endorse the summoning of these entities and so have not included the formula on how to summon them. It's never that easy and is highly dangerous without the proper knowledge.

EVIL IS IN EVERY CULTURE

ere, we are going to talk about evil entities from different religions, no belief system is exempt from negative forms, however most other cultures do not refer to their negative entities as demons, but as evil spirits. Although I do not regularly get calls for exorcisms of evil spirits, a demonologist always needs to be prepared, by studying various religious beliefs and entities—this has enabled me to help people from almost every religion. Different belief systems contain different spirits and ways to rid oneself of them, you will notice some of these entities used to actually be human, humans turning evil or being eternally tortured after death is not a concept unfamiliar to any belief system. In Christianity, if you are a good person and stick to the commandments, you go to heaven; if you have done evil you go to hell. With many of today's religious belief systems, the definition may not be so clear; some spirits are looking for revenge, others help, and still others are getting their karmic punishment as it were. So even though technically they are not considered demons, they are highly negative, entities that often have similar patterns to demonic entities.

Now not all of the beings contained herein were previously human, some of them are atypical of a demonic entity and by their very nature alone would be included within the category. So let's just take a trip around the world to see what evil lies in different cultures.

BUDDHISM AND SHINTO

Lets first begin in the Japanese culture, which mainly practices Buddhism and Shinto, although they never specify belonging to one specific religion but often meld or borrow from both. Shinto in particular is specific only to Japan where it was first practiced. They refer to their gods as Kami. It is an earth-based religion which holds that rocks, trees, and nature itself holds spirit. Humans actually become Kami after they die and are worshipped by their family because of it, so often you will find elaborate family shrines. Within Japanese religion lies what they call Yomi, where ones soul goes to deteriorate and rot for eternity; it is not based on how you behaved but seen as just the way of things. Once a soul has eaten in Yomi, you are confined there indefinitely. In between Yomi and the physical world is a no-soul's land, where distressed and negative spirits roam. Shinto is a predominantly positive faith and does not believe there is any right or wrong, and understands that we are not meant to be perfect, but we are essentially good. However, they do also observe polarities in the Kami. Such as the Oni.

Oni

Considered to be neutral they have the power to bring destruction or blessings upon a person or house. Also in Japan Oni can constitute as a stranger or outsider. Onis were originally thought to be invisible, however, over the generations and influences of other cultures they gained the form of misshapen creatures. The negative Oni is also referred to as evil Kami, which suggests that Oni is as worshipped as it is feared. These evil entities would bring disaster, plaque, and death. Later in time, through much influence from the Chinese, those who practiced Shinto began to believe that by using peaches (which in the Chinese culture supposedly rids of any evil or toxic spirit), they could ward off or rid themselves of the evil Kami. There are many ceremonies held during the year giving offerings to the Oni to appease them.

As I said earlier, I don't often get calls to deal with evil entities from other cultures but, luckily, I was prepared when I got a phone call from a Buddhist girl who claimed she had a hungry spirit. So next let us talk about them. You have seen this type of entity before if you have ever seen the movie *The Grudge*. However, most Hungry Spirits are not as graphic or malignant as portrayed within the movie; but they are still considered evil. Below is some information about the Hungry Spirit including the case I worked.

Hungry Spirits

I recently dealt with a woman who had a hungry spirit. I thought the term hungry spirit or hungry ghost was specific to the Buddhist religion, but while researching this entity, I realized it permeates not only Buddhism but Hinduism, Roman Paganism, Taoism, and it is touched on in the *Book of Enoch*.

Taoists feel that hungry spirits are actually the ghosts of people that did not receive everything they needed to survive in the afterlife, so it comes back to our world to feed off us! They will feed off your energy and fear.

They also believe that the way a building is structured can affect whether or not you are prone to attracting hungry spirits, offering food and other things will help to appease these spirits. In the *Book of Enoch* it talks about how they believed Hungry Spirits were the result of the mating between humans and watchers or fallen angels. These entities supposedly wander the world as evil spirits always wanting food though they have no mouths and cannot eat, constantly thirsty though they cannot drink. They are the most envious of the living and always seek to have what we have. They possess weak-willed men and women to take over their bodies so they can eat and drink. Buddhist priests often pray with the afflicted but do not aim to harm, or chase away the spirit as they believe there is a block or grudge on both sides and aim to help both spirit and afflicted to be released from their issues.

To protect our clients, I will be using first initials only. We were called into a case where a hungry spirit haunted a Vietnamese couple, every time M bought food, the next day the rice would go bad, sometimes the vegetables as well. The grain would be filled with maggots and browned.

When we entered the apartment, the smell was fierce, like someone had left trash to fester. The small apartment was clean and tidy, however, when we looked in the cabinets, there was the rice, maggots and all. We spent the next half hour scouring the apartment for a cause of the rice and vegetables going bad, but none could be found.

I had prepared seals for everyone to protect themselves. Raven and Beckah felt that the seals were prohibiting them from reading, but another member of our crew at the time, a psychic artist, kept hers on. She mentioned it warmed when we entered the apartment. I carried on me a seal different from the others; it was to command and compel spirits to do my bidding, and obviously we all wanted this one gone.

Beckah and Raven did their walkthroughs confirming my suspicions of the entity—there had been discord within M and E which attracted the spirit. The seal I carried depicted a scorpion in the center. As our psychic artist walked through the apartment picking up images, I began helping M start the process of banishing the entity.

We stood in the living room while the artist was in the bedroom, I held the seal for M to see, then continued with incantations that bound the entity to do the will of the person who held the seal. It was a matter of minutes before the spirit had departed and M began to put holy water on windows, faucets, electronic outlets, and other sources through which the spirit could return. She used the holy water to paint the symbol of her faith on each door as well. We left for a couple of minutes so M and E could feel the difference in their home. When we returned, they admitted that there was more light in their apartment than before, it felt easier to move, and they felt more clear headed.

Our psychic artist took the opportunity to show the sketches she had drawn. First was a woman, her jaw wide open and slack at the same time, her eyes looked hollow and her hair was dirty; she was obviously in pain. The second was of arguments in the living room and fighting. The third was of a mask on the bedroom wall, scorpions coming our of its mouth and spreading throughout the house. I was amazed at this, I had never used a seal around our artist but it was another form of confirmation for me that reinforced the belief in my system. Our artist had never seen my seal, I went home with the knowledge that M and E would be alright. We have talked with M and E since; they have split up as a couple, but amicably, and neither has had any more trouble with hungry spirits.

Have you ever watched the movie *The Grudge*? Have you seen the sequel? If you haven't seen the sequel to it, first of all, it was an awesome movie, secondly, it gives a good example of a hungry spirit. At one point, there is a character who is possessed by one of these entities and she drinks a half gallon of milk; she then proceeds to throw it up back into the bottle and drink it again. When possessed by hungry spirits, phenomena such as thist isn't uncommon. These spirits are dangerous and can lead to death.

Yurei
The Japanese culture has some beliefs that are specific to no religion at all but show a cosmic truth and common thought about the afterlife contained within all religions. The Yurei shows this as it is believed to be a spirit not put to rest. They do not wander, but stay in the same area (such as where their body is buried or where they died), or follow a specific person (such as their murderer or loved one). The Japanese feel that the veil between worlds is thinnest between the hours of two and three a.m. and so this is the only time when the Yurei is visible. The spirits usually have a specific purpose, and the best way to rid yourself of one is to help them fulfill it.

Onry
These spirits are typically women who were powerless during their lives and gain it once they die. They are often fueled by the need for revenge, jealousy, or greed, although their form of revenge is not on the husband, but the town, or new wife. Although there is one infamous story of Oiwa where after death she went after the husband—though not looking to kill, but rather torment the man psychologically. The girl from the movie *The Ring* would be considered an Onry.

ISLAMIC
Islam is the second most popular faith in the world with a following of over one billion people called Muslims. The word Islam literally translates to "Submission to God" hence why "a Muslim is one who strives to submit to God." Islam dictates that whatever happens is the will of Allah, and that even with the Jinni they will go so far as Allah will allow them. Unlike the Christian faiths who believe there was a Holy War in Heaven and that Lucifer was cast out, Islam has a different take on this. They believe Allah created Adam out of black clay like mud.

He then told his angels that when he had finished breathing the soul into his new creation, they should all lie prostrate before him. When the time came, Iblis (Lucifer/Satan) refused; they struck a bargain that Iblis would be allowed to return on the Day of Recompense, but during this time he swore to befuddle and lead astray man from the true path of God. Allah allowed Iblis to take some people with him. There was no mention of fallen angels.

Jinn

These spirits were created by Allah out of a smokeless fire before He created Adam. They are an invisible race that is in between the Angels and Man. They have the ability to manifest into anything they choose, and their powers of illusion are very strong. It is believed that the Jinni inhabit ruins or abandoned homes and like to be near fire, so they may choose to stay near a home's hearth. It is believed that they are the cause of sandstorms. The Islamic peoples also believe that each section of land has its own spirit and so they ask permission to enter an area instead of just walking right in. There are many stories about the Jinn, good and bad, but it is believed that you should leave them alone because you would never know which is good and which is bad until it is to late. For a simple explanation of Jinni classes, we looked to an authority:

Ibn Abdul Barr said, "The jinn, according to the scholars of the language, are of different types:

- If one is mentioning the jinn purely of themselves, the are called *jinni*.
- If one is mentioning the jinn that live among mankind, they are called *aamar* whose plural is *amaar*.
- If one is mentioning the ones that antagonize the young, they are called *arwaah*.
- If one is mentioning the evil ones that antagonize humans, they are called *shaitan* for the singular [and *shayateen* for plural].
- If they cause even more harm and become strong, they are called *afreet*."

~The World of the Jinn
and Devils, p. 7

The Islamic people recognize Jinni as a completely separate race, that can be converted to their faith, be shown a good way to live and thrive within a community. They can also be even tempered, mischievous, or so mild you never even know they are there. Shaitan on the other hand (also known as Satan) is Iblis and his people, they are inherently evil; they are there for the sole purpose of getting followers and true believers of Allah to sin, by any means necessary. Many of them create the illusion of looking human when trying to tempt and can take on the form of friends, family, or a stranger in need of help. They can also take the form of animals and have been known to possess both dead bodies and sometimes living people. Much like the Christian demons, many have an extreme negative reaction to water of any type, especially that which is blessed.

ABORIGINAL AUSTRALIA

Let's now move more southerly, very, very southerly. To Australia; aboriginals still inhabit the island continent and so do the evil spirits they fear. They have a deep sense of connectedness with the Earth believing that from a rock to a tree to a person, they are all part of the same spirit. The Aboriginal spirituality is just that, a spirituality, each with their own concepts, beliefs, and stories. They often gain spiritual knowledge during what is called "The Dreaming" which is the time between waking and sleeping, when they feel they have the strongest connection to the ancestors and earth spirits. During the Dreaming, they also form their archetypes, realize their totems, find songs or chants and ceremonies, and so their Dreaming could also be considered a mythology. Some of the Aboriginal language is not able to be translated into English because it has never been a written language, only an oral one, so Dreaming is a loose term for the state they enter when collecting information from spirit. Evil spirits are mainly a part of their oral history and are tied into their mythology, and so in order to depict these entities correctly, we must review some of the Aboriginal oral stories.

Gabba Gabba

Within the community, the oral tradition talks about how the world was made and the entity known as Gabba Gabba occupied the Red Cliffs, now known as Woolloogabba (it is also known as "The Fighting Place"). Kalbarri aborigines claim that the evil entity is still around and causing violence in the area. Unfortunately, due to a lack of information on this and other entities within the Aboriginal culture, there is not much that can be told.

Mamu

Mamu is a type of evil entity believed to travel the deserts in Australia; they eat men without even thinking. They are shape shifters and will change into anything, from people you know, to animals, to objects you may carry upon your person or find out in the desert—anything to get close enough to kill you. When in their true form, they are described as gruesome creatures with angular faces, a large mouth, and pointed ears. Fire is supposedly a great deterrent for these entities. Mamu also means "evil spirit" or "malignant being" and so this word has been used to describe many types of Aboriginal entities.

HINDUISM

Let's go somewhere a little more exotic. Why don't we go check on India and Hinduism—this belief system is often claimed to be the oldest of the modern religions. It is often called Sanatana Darhma translating to "the eternal way" or "eternal law." There are six branches of the religion, the first being the folk religion which is usually carried by oral tradition—they worship local deities and entities. There is the Vedic tradition, which is based in the Vedas or recorded scripture (specifically the Rig Veda). The third is Vedantic which relies mainly upon the Upishands, a collection of scriptures that Shankara had written commentaries about back in the eighth century; it is a following and worship of the core principals of the Upishands, which refers to individual spirits and universal spirit. These scriptures do not pertain to any particular time during Sanskrit literature, the earliest dating back to the Brahamana period during the first millenium BCE. The fourth tradition (and last that we will mention here) is the Yogic, often represented by the sutras of Patañjali which is an intense system of connection with the universal spirit of God through meditation and metaphysics. Hinduism has no founder or one person who started the religious way, but many people, if you read over their sacred texts, refer to both men and women who look at the world in a scientific-like view, but still retain a strong sense of spirituality—which means they too had their demons and evil spirits.

Asuras

The Indo-Aryan's holy book, called the Rig Veda, contained within its pages mention of Asuras, which originally meant any type of spirit—didn't matter if they were good or evil. So most of the demi-gods and devas held the title of Asura. However, the Indo-Aryans soon changed the meaning of the word to mean any one of a race of evil entities with human-like features, though they are disfigured and hideous. They are considered to be demonic entities. These demons are always in battle with the demi-gods and gods, which is why they are commonly depicted carrying weaponry to battle with the Asuras. Unlike other major religions, the Indo-Aryans do not believe Asuras are the cause of evil within our current society, but rather formations created by the immoral wants in our consciousness. Asuras, unlike demi-gods or devas, are mortal, although they yearn for everlasting life. The Hindu religion has strong beliefs in reincarnation and changes of the soul depending on Karma. If a human is extremely horrible in this life, their soul upon their death will turn into an evil ghostly spirit. However, these Asuras are considered as being from *Naraka,* the lower plane, and they can repent and be elevated to goodness.

Vetalas

There are many different types of these spirits that are recognized by the Hindu religion, such as Vetalas which are vampire-like evil spirits that can possess corpses; they tend to haunt cemeteries. The Vetala is known to cause miscarriages, kill children, and drive people insane. The only way to rid oneself is to give them funeral rites; to repel them, you need to use holy mantras.

Pishachas

Pishachas which are flesh eating entities, although no one is sure where they came from, tend to haunt cremation grounds. They will also possess a person causing them to become insane or cause another form of sickness. The Pishachas are given offerings at certain festivals to keep them away, but some mantras are used to cure the possessed victim of this particular Hindu spirit.

JUDAISM

The Hebrew actually does not acknowledge any demonic entities, but they do accept the presence of evil spirits.

Incubus/Succubus

Incubus means "to lie upon" in Latin—supposedly these demon lovers preyed upon women. Succubus, which means "to lie beneath," preyed on the men. They were believed to take human form at night, sometimes even looking like the victim's spouse or lover. Both demons had the ability to paralyze their mates and to cause a whole household to fall into almost sleep- or catatonic-like states while there. During the later Middle Ages, it was actually believed the Incubus and Succubus were the same entity that took on different manifestations according to their victim's sex. But where does this belief come from? Well, it actually dates back to the time of the Assyrian's and Lilith (Lilis).

Lilis/Lilith

Lilith was supposed to be Adam's first love, however, because she would not accept being beneath him, she was banished. Later, she was known as the Night Hag—she herself was a sexual demon; scorned, she tried to gain vengeance on the human race by mating with men. The children that she spawned from her victims were called Lili; they roamed the night satisfying their lust with men. Lilis (Lilith) visits the bedrooms of women who have recently had babies, to kill them out of spite. She waits eight days for the boys and twenty-one for the girls before she begins her murderous endeavors. To chase this demon away, draw circles on the wall of the room with charcoal and within each write, "Adam, Eve, Lilis, Avaunt." On the door to the room, write the name of the three angels of medicine, Senoi, Sanmangelof, and Sansenoi. Apparently, according to angelic history, the art of medicine was taught to these three angels by Lilis.

Dybbuk

This is the term used for a lost soul that attaches itself to a human person with the intent of completing a task it was not able to finish in life. Dybbuk is a Hebrew word meaning "clinging." These spirits are attracted to a person who is in a similar situation or mindset as the dybbuk was in life. But it is important to note that not all dybbuks come with intent to harm or hurt, or even to complete a task. There are some times when the dybbuk comes to actually help a person who is in a situation similar to theirs—one that the dybbuk was able to overcome, but the person isn't. So in that instance, they act like a guide.

NEGATIVE THOUGHTFORMS

hat is a thoughtform? This type of entity is actually a buildup of negative energy created from a single or group of people's emotions and thoughts. Usually created during times of argument, depression, stress, or all of these emotions at once. We have to remember that our mind and our emotions are powerful tools and that we can manifest entities without being aware of it. If you know what you are doing, you can create a powerful thoughtform within a couple of weeks, however, for those who are unaware of the creature they have manifested, it could take a lot longer.

Oftentimes, a thoughtform will present itself as a dark figure or cloud; it can only be destroyed by the one who created it. Imagine, you're on a cliff looking into a swirling black void; it's filled with hate, anger, and sadness. This is a thoughtform; it is an extension of yourself. However, more than once it has been confused with the demonic because of the way it will manifest its appearance. Some people have claimed to see coil-like black clouds, full-figured men in robes, animal-like figures, or themselves (except all in black). Basically, a thoughtform will take on whatever scares you the most because once it has a mind of its own; it wants to feed off your emotions, whether you are willing or not.

To destroy a thoughtform is difficult for a couple of reasons; one, typically it cannot be seen, although it can be felt; and two, it is an aspect of the person, and their negative emotions, hate, anger, and fear is a hard thing to face. But it can be done! Counseling will often help with thoughtforms because the more you work through your issues, the less the thoughtform will have to feed. So when confronting it directly, even if you can't see it, do not try to just kick it out of your home, workplace, or life. That will not work. When confronted like that the entity will engulf you with the pain and anger you and others have fed it. The one thing you have to remember is you cannot be afraid—there is no reason to be; this creature is YOU!

Sometimes, you will walk into a house and feel the negativity seeping out of the walls. That usually means there is a thoughtform of some kind living there. A thoughtform will affect you even if it was not created by you. It will draw whatever negative emotion you possess to the forefront of your mind. You may think about arguments from twenty or thirty years ago; you may remember embarrassing moments, or moments of fear and pain. This is all for a reason! Think of it this way: When you are vacuuming a floor, does the vacuum care what it is sucking up? No! Neither does a thoughtform. More often than not, when leaving a property possessed by a thoughtform, you will feel drained, dizzy, out of sorts. Some people even claim to have black-out periods. During this time, arguments will take place, slander, fist fighting—this is just another way thoughtforms will use you to create the drama it needs to feed.

Here is an example from one of my cases:

I was called to an apartment rented by two couples living there together. Before they moved in, they were the best of friends. However, two of the roommates suffered from severe depression and mood swings. I decided to sit these two women down and find out what was really going on. They both described their lives growing up; one was the daughter of a real estate lawyer, the other of a single mom. Both started with depression in their teen years and had been in and out of counseling since. For Jane, the daughter of the real estate lawyer, when the medications and therapy didn't work for her depression, she turned to drugs. Things spiraled downhill with her for the next two or three years till her father forced her to go to a rehabilitation center in California. There she met her husband who was also fighting addiction; they graduated the program within a week of each other. Their first apartment was small. Over time, Jane began to feel the depression again and things steadily grew worse. She couldn't sleep, she had nightmares all the time, she was constantly fighting with her husband over small things, she claimed she thought she was psychic because she saw a ghost all the time in her apartment. I just nodded my head not really sure whether it was a demonic entity, negative spirit, or thoughtform because the things she was telling me could be any one of those entities. I hoped with the other woman I would get more details or clues.

"I think I have a thoughtform." said Kerry, the daughter of the single mother. "I have suffered from depression for years, all while growing up, and the past three years, I kind of just got stuck in it. I see figures out of the corner of my eye; they scare me, almost like black clouds that are about to take shape into something else. But I always get so scared I look away. I still lived with my mother at the time and we used to argue to no end; I would break out in tears for nothing. When I would tell it to leave me alone, I would get angry. I broke plates and cups in a fit of rage one time! When I moved in with my boyfriend, things got better; I was happy. But then we moved in with this couple. I thought what I went through when I was with my mother was bad. I was wrong. This has been horrible!"

"I understand that, but what makes you think you have a thoughtform?" I asked.

"Well, I am really into the New Age stuff. I thought maybe getting back into a spirituality would help the issue, but it hasn't. Anyway, one day I was reading a book and it talked about thoughtforms—it fit this situation exactly!"

"Alright, thank you," I said. I then asked for all four to sit down with me to discuss what was currently going on in the apartment.

They claimed a feeling of being followed by a threatening presence. One husband was in the Navy and talked about recurring flashbacks and feelings of intense negative emotion towards his wife and roommates. They also said they felt wonderful outside the home, but being inside was a drain; the only time they felt any energy at all was when they were arguing or upset.

That did it for me, I knew then we were dealing with a thoughtform, not a demonic entity or negative spirit—because demonic and spirits will follow you throughout the day, whereas thoughtforms will stick to where the most negative energy is.

I decided to smudge the house with sage to clear any excess of negativity the entity could feed upon. From here, I asked both women if they were currently attending counseling; they weren't. I advised they go back into it to work on the issues they were currently having; meanwhile, they confronted the monster. I conjured the thoughtform into a circle—it was massive, as though two thoughtforms had joined to create one huge one. I made Jane and Kerry stand in front of the thoughtform (although outside the circle, so they wouldn't get hurt). The two women asked the entity a variety of personal questions, about their lives, their hate, anger, depression; both realized what they considered a negative thoughtform, was nothing but themselves, their silent suffering wanting to be heard. As they talked to the thoughtform for the next hour, you could see it like an onion—the layers kept peeling back. It grew smaller and smaller, as the girls came to terms with the reasons for its creation. Finally, like a piece of lint, it blew away.

These two women are still currently in counseling and decided to leave the apartment, each wanting their own space while they worked on their healing.

Thoughtforms, when created out of a feeling of fear can actually both scare and protect the individual it is attached to. Here is an example from my cases.

A Case Study

I was called by a mother of a teenage daughter—during and right after puberty, female children are at the height of their abilities for manifestation and psychic ability. She said her child was being terrorized by the ghost of a man dressed all in white with a cape or robe. He would appear in the doorways and windows of the home and knock on the walls next to her head at night when she was trying to fall asleep. This girl did not have a history of depression or anger issues, so before I arrived I thought it was probably just a negative spirit. When I reached their home, I could feel the negativity around me. *Okay, a negative entity*, I thought. *I'm going to keep an open mind on this one!*

I went into the living room with the girl—her name was Constance. Her dark hair hung below her shoulders, her jeans hung a little loose, and her shirt was oversized. Self-esteem and body issues I figured. In a monotone voice, she told me of her experiences, "I'm thirteen and home schooled. Ever since I started thinking about going back to public school this guy has been showing up. He's not scary, but the way he appears, disappears, makes noise, that frightens me."

"What happened that you left school the first time?" I asked.

"I was teased horribly; you know, once one girl starts to pick on you, then they all do. All my friends turned into enemies; I was a complete outcast within the first year at school. These are people I had been friends with since I was little and I just didn't understand. One day I was sitting at the table with them in the cafeteria, and the next, I was by myself, or sneaking up to the library during lunch. People would call me fat, and other mean names, I just couldn't take it. No matter how hard I tried to fight back, it just made it worse. Like I said, though I have been thinking about going back over this past month or so, and since then this guy, he looks like an albino almost, he won't leave me alone."

"So is it fair to say you have been too scared to go back? Maybe depressed that you couldn't fix the problem?" Figures were adding up in my head, even though the entity didn't look like the typical thoughtform, maybe it was.

"Totally, I am completely terrified to return, and I have been depressed because I lost all my friends—I am cut off here. I haven't spoken to anyone from school since the day Mom took me out." She kept looking down at her hands and fiddling with her fingers; she was nervous and scared. "Then knocks started; bangs were more like it. Wind chimes hung inside the house began moving."

"Are you scared right now?" I asked Constance.

"Uh-huh." She sat on the couch with me watching the activity. "I don't know what to do, or think. Part of me wants to keep it here; I feel safe in a weird way, but also like I'm in prison, and there is no hope."

BINGO! I needed to help her face her fear. Over the next month, her mother did as I asked by getting her into counseling. By the end of the second month, Constance was feeling ready to go back to school. On that morning, I came to her house to see her off. This case had gotten to me; what she had said resonated with some of my own experiences from childhood. I waved goodbye and told her to call me if she was scared or needed anything. As she walked down the driveway, the entity stood in front of her. Silently it looked at her, as if waiting for something. Then it all clicked for Constance, it was here to help her and just reflected whatever she was feeling at the moment. If she was scared, it made noise, if she was lonely it appeared, if she felt hopeless, it wanted everyone to feel it.

"I don't need you anymore," she said softly, she looked it right in the eye.

She kept on walking, and never looked back. Since then, Constance's problems at school have lessened and she has reached honors for the past three years; she is now in high school and loving it. The albino thoughtform has not been seen since.

Negative thoughtforms can cause a lot of problems in your life, ranging from just having the feeling you are not alone, to causing your car to break down, unlucky streaks, losing your job, and so on. It's Law of Attraction at work, if you think positive, you will attract positive entities and creates positive thoughtforms, if you think negative, well, the opposite will happen.

It also happens that sometimes a negative thoughtform will be sent either consciously or unconsciously to another person. This actually happened to one of my spouse's friends. Jen, the poor woman, had just gotten a divorce from an abusive husband and was renting out a top floor apartment in Hooksett for her and her daughter. Within three days of moving, Jen got a letter from her attorney saying he was dropping her case. Flabbergasted, she searched through the phone book for a new attorney. Finally, she found another with the same degree of skill as her prior one. That night, after Jen tucked her daughter into bed, the phone rang. She picked it up, but all she heard was heavy breathing on the other end.

The way she had left her husband wasn't normal. Her friend parked outside the house at night while her spouse was at work, then Jen packed her and the daughter's bags and left the house. She did leave a note simply stating, "I want a divorce." The next morning, she called into work and got a hold of the attorney.

So the night of the phone call Jen stayed up, worried that her husband had found her. The next morning, over tea, she told her friend about the call. After about a half hour of talking, Jen walked away a lot calmer. She took a week off work to spend with her daughter. The time flew by as they traveled around the town, went to restaurants and movies. She arrived home one Sunday afternoon to find the front door ajar. She called for her friend but there was no answer, so she stayed outside the home and called the police. They couldn't find anyone in the house or any sign of break in.

Jen had her own ideas. Throughout the next month she became paranoid and depressed, even though her lawyer told her that her husband has been in Michigan with family since she left. She lost her job, her car, Jen's friend's marriage was breaking up, her daughter was having nightmares, and she couldn't sleep. After about five or six months of suffering, she asked my spouse for a reading. When we met up with her, it was obvious that she was having some extreme issues. She had dark circles under her eyes, she'd lost weight, and she looked like death warmed over.

My spouse ignored the cards and began pacing the kitchen. Then she turned to Jen and said, "Who's the man your daughter has been seeing." Jen turned pale, her eyes wide. "My daughter has been dreaming of her father, except he is all black ooze like oil."

My spouse asked if she has been experiencing any paranormal activity. "No, but I have been forgetting things lately; like just yesterday, I could have sworn I closed the door to my apartment, but when I came home, it was wide open and so was my bedroom window, which I also thought I closed. When I first moved in, I know I closed the door to the house, but when I came home it too was wide open and I called the cops. But they said that I must have left it open because there was no sign of break in or anyone being inside the home. I thought it was my husband and that he had found me, but he would have left something for me to know he was there, and he's been in Michigan since I left. Every time I have a happy moment, something horrible happens. One day I'm enjoying myself shopping with my daughter, the next I lost my job. When I asked why, all they told me was that it was my attendance—but they okayed the days I took off! Oh, not to mention that my car broke down; thank God in heaven that my friend is letting me stay here rent free or I would be screwed."

Jen's cheeks were wet with tears, her heart was open, and she was looking for healing. We decided to check out the apartment upstairs. Immediately we knew something was up. My spouse felt a highly negative presence in the apartment, looking around, she kept spotting it out of the corner of her eye—a thick coil of black smoke, specific to a thoughtform. The psychic went to Jen's room and touched the bed; she saw Jen's husband forcing himself on her. Dreams and memories from Jen's past flooded the psychic, tears streamed down her face at the horrors the woman had dealt with.

My spouse looked at me, "It's a thoughtform, created by both of their pain; he hates her, deeply, and sent the thing here. I don't think he knows about it though. Her pain and anguish has fed it since then, it has grown very, very large and is engulfing this home. If we don't get rid of it, things are going to get a lot worse, quick."

They both headed downstairs and told Jen what they had figured out; the woman let out a sigh of relief. "Do you think after you take this thing out that my life will get back to normal?" A look of hope infused Jen's face.

"It should," I said, "but we can't just get rid of it, you have to face it, face your fear, your anger, your husband's anger—let it know it can't affect you anymore, that you know it exists and it has no power." Jen nodded in acceptance of my counsel and took a moment to prepare herself for the most important battle of her life.

We ascended the stairs; Jen trembled with nervousness and my spouse put a reassuring hand on her shoulder. We went directly to the bedroom and Jen called out to the entity, "I know you are here, I know what you are, you can't hurt me anymore!" The windows slammed open.

"You can't scare me, I'm protected by God! Derek, he hurt me! I will not stand to have you in my home! I forgive him for what he did to me, but I will not forget! I release you from this home; go away!" Jen's trembling got worse, my spouse hugged her and moved to the left of her just as the entity came by us. "Go away! I don't want you here! I don't need you! I pity him! I release my pain, I give it to God! You have no power over me! GET OUT!" Jen roared. The room began to lighten and we smiled as we watched the black form dissipate.

"It's gone," I said with a big sigh of relief. I looked over at Jen who stood still in my spouse's arm tears sliding down her face.

The next day we came over her house, Katie cleansed the entire building, to make sure there were no more stagnant negative energies that could build up to create another thoughtform. She gave Jen the instructions and told her to do it every couple of months to make sure that through this hard divorce another entity didn't form. A week later, Katie called Jen, she hadn't gotten a job yet, but her husband was going to give her the house and the bulk of their stock and bonds. She wouldn't have to worry about working for a while. Derek had apologized for everything he had done to her, her daughter no longer has nightmares, and Jen hasn't been paranoid since.

SPECIFICS ON THOUGHTFORMS

Thoughts—we think them everyday—but I didn't realize how powerful they were until I came upon my first thoughtform, and since, I have never forgotten. Millions suffer from thoughtform infestation without ever knowing the causes. Here I am going to give you a list, but be aware, when it comes to negative entities, they each have the same goal to torment and destroy you and their methods are sometimes similar. So before jumping the gun, please get someone who knows what they are doing to investigate it.

SIGNS AND SYMPTOMS OF A THOUGHTFORM

- Black smoke, curly cues, or figures typically out of the corner of the eye
- Poltergeist activity, particularly opening and closing things
- Constant fatigue
- Nightmares, typically of your greatest fear, either person, place, or thing.
- Loss of job, car, child (not dead but taken away)
- Streak of bad luck (everything you do goes bad)
- Depression
- Thoughts of suicide
- Friends seem to turn against you
- A sudden unreasonable fear or phobia
- If a thoughtform is sent to you, you will think about that person all the time.
- Your business transactions will go bad (one day you have $1,000 in your checking account, the next by some screw up you will be minus twice that.)

Though the list is short, it displays the most commons signs of a thoughtform. Look out for them; these entities are more common than negative spirits and demonic combine.

SPIRITS UNDER SIEGE

here are those times that demonic entities will use spirits for help to terrorize homes and individuals. These spirits are not always negative ones and sometimes are forced to create poltergeist activity in a home or business. Demonic entities need to cause a distraction so that their plans can be carried out. There are also times when a demonic entity will use a spirit's energy to draw power; this will amplify the demonic power. In cases such as these, I will ask my spouse (who is a psychic medium) to assist me. While I am working on the demonic entities, the psychic is helping those spirits break free from their demonic hold and then they can safely cross over. This is never an easy task, for the demonic will never just let go of a spirit without a fight.

This is a dangerous business. not just for myself and the psychic, but the spirit as well. It is like being trapped in a building by a vicious killer. Yes, the police have him surrounded, but the killer may decide to get rid of you anyway. A demonic entity would rather get rid of the spirits than let them go. So protecting them as well as others in the house is a priority, because even though the spirits may have caused some form of harm, they are not necessarily at fault. Oftentimes, these scenarios work to the benefit of both the client and spirit.

I am an Occultist at heart, so the steps I take are based around the signs and sigils used to trap an inhuman spirit; they are also known as wards. I will corner the entity by laying out a sigil—usually there is a bit of ruckus that occurs right before they are caught. Then the psychic will attempt contact with the spirits. This will happen quickly as time may be short, depending on the strength of the demon. It is made sure that the medium is protected; through education and field work the psychics in my crew have developed their own system to discern spirit from inhuman. The medium will cross over as many spirits as she can in the limited amount of time we have.

If the demonic does break the seal, it will be ticked, and will have no issue letting us know. When dealing with these beings, science will not often come into play—we must fight fire with fire. This process of trapping, releasing spirits, and counterattack could go on for more than an hour; usually no longer than that though, as the longer we continue the event, the more we are tired and the entity more enraged. It all comes down to assessment of the situation and following instinct.

Although demons have their own power, their own source of energy, they will usually rely on spirits to stir up the beginnings of trouble and later to reenergize them when they over extend their abilities. So the more spirits we help cross over, the less souls for them and the less energy they can use. It works out for everyone—except the demon of course.

But just because a spirit is enslaved by a demon, this does not give it any extra abilities it didn't have before. Spirits will manifest in whatever way the demonic entity wants, however, their abilities are limited. They can only move small objects and they don't transport things. However, they may slide a chair across the floor. They may appear as dark shadows, and out of your peripheral vision, as a black cloud which can often be confused with demonic entities. Spirits will write things on the mirrors or create patterns; you can also hear their voices clearly when they would like to make contact, almost like a whisper. Spirits do not typically cause rape-like feeling as demons do, however, they will stand over your bed and can sometimes cause you to feel the effects of their death, such as suffocation or heart attack. But this is not typically meant in a harmful way, but is another way of spirit communication.

As with demonic entities, smells can be present, however, it is not usually that of garbage or feces, but of a smell relative to the deceased, such as cigars, a certain brand of perfume, flowers, etc. I am not saying that all spirits are pleasant, just like not every person is pleasant, but typically, the only time a spirit gets violent is either when it is being controlled or not being heard—the latter usually results in poltergeist activity.

A spirit under siege is a painful thing—for the psychic, demonologist, victim and spirit. Most of these poor souls are trapped in an abyss of pain and torment. So when you next come across a spirit in a position such as this, be aware of the circumstances, because it could be a member of the victim's family or someone with no original intent to harm but caught in the wrong place and wrong time. These poor souls have no say in what they do and how they act; they do not have the ability to break free of their bonds, just as most victims of demonic influence, they don't know they are in trouble till it is to late.

SPIRIT IN TERROR

A woman called me around one a.m.; I always keep a phone by the bed just in case, she was crying and asking for help. I woke my spouse up to make a pot of coffee while I tried to calm the woman down. I sat on the edge of the bed listening to her erratic speech, mentioning something about demons and evil in her house. I have to admit I am the type of person that is not awake before coffee, but hearing this woman woke me up like I had already had a pot.

I kept trying to ask her name, but again she was hysterical. Finally, I asked her where she lived and she quickly gave me directions, it was about an hour away and I told her I would be there as soon as I could. I came out to the kitchen, looked at my spouse who was waiting for the pot to finish brewing and said, "We're going to need the travel mugs."

After about fifteen minutes, we were on the road. The radio in my car was silent; I was just thinking about what I could make out the woman saying. She mentioned she was alone in her home, she had gone to bed around ten-ish as was her ritual since becoming an empty nester. She mentioned something about a door slamming downstairs two or three times and then hearing footsteps up the stairs, and a picture of her mother flying off of her dresser.

Finally, we got there; the house was rather large, all the lights were on, and the woman was sitting on her front steps. She had a roll of toilet paper next to her and was holding the broken picture of her mother. I greeted her, and introduced my spouse. It was as if she didn't even see me there; she was very distraught. After about ten minutes, I got her to recognize we were standing there and then she was okay.

It took some convincing, but we eventually got her to come back into the house. We sat down in the living room and talked. She said her name was Jo-anne and then calmly stated there was a demon in the house. I asked how she knew this and she said her mother told her. I looked around for the mom but Jo-anne informed me the mother was in fact dead.

"My mother was sensitive," she told us. "She promised that after she died, she would stay in the house with me and watch over me and the kids. My last one just left for college and this is the first time I've had to be alone since the divorce."

"How long ago was that?" I asked.

"About six years ago," Jo-anne replied.

"So how do you think the demon got here?" I asked.

"Well, like I said my mother was sensitive to spirits; almost everyone in my family had some kind of ability and her friends were all into that kind of thing. So was my grandmother, but not like my mother was. She used to hold séances upstairs in the attic, but she never let me go down into the basement either. After my mother died, I couldn't even think of coming back into the house. However, after my divorce, I didn't really have a choice. I haven't changed much; anyway I went down into the basement to make some room for my big pieces of furniture and I found all sorts of stuff that I had seen when she used to do the séances. Her table was down there and it had some odd carvings in it, I think they made the table into a giant Ouija Board, but aside from that, she also had crystal balls, decks of cards, and little crystals on strings. I put it all in a corner of the basement, but while I was looking through it, I remembered one time when Mom was trying to get in touch with the spirit of my uncle and she got really angry because he kept saying he couldn't. She pressed as to why and he said other things; I only remember that because two days later, Mom had a priest over to bless the house. My uncle has always been a protective spirit in the home; I used to see him when I was little, but since that day, I didn't really see him anymore. I thought maybe it was because I was growing up, but with everything that has happened now, I don't know, maybe he was trying to protect me."

"Why are you so convinced it's demonic?" I inquired.

"Like I said, my mother told me so, there have been little things ever since I could remember. For example, one time when I was around ten, I tried to sneak into the basement to find out what was going on down there and I heard a dog growling at me, like he was standing right in front of me. Umm, oh yeah, another time I was working on a project for high school and I saw this black figure out of the corner of my eye, and one day I woke up to get ready for school, went back into my room, and found my cross necklace had gone missing. I found it later in the séance room. I figured maybe my mother had tried to use it for something because it had been a gift from my uncle to her and then she gave it to me. Another time, we had a spiritualist here, and he was trying to help my mom get in touch with someone—I don't remember who, but next thing I know he fell down the stairs with a *thunk*. He claims he was pushed and he never came back to the house. I remember Mom was mad about that because he didn't get in touch with who she had wanted and he charged her a lot of money for it."

"Well, if you don't mind I'm going to take a look around the house and see what we can do for you," I said. She agreed and I asked my spouse to stay with her and keep her company, so she didn't feel so scared or alone. I started upstairs in the attic where the séances were held; it was pretty empty, but the room felt full, like walking through snow. The wood floor was very worn, and every once in a while I could see flecks of paint. I bent down for closer inspection. The attic was unfinished and there was no paint to be seen. I found what looked like some type of glyph, but I wasn't sure quite what it was. I noticed them in different colors all around the middle of the floor, but again they were too worn away to tell exactly what they were supposed to be. From what little I could tell, the symbols were in a perfect circle, which might—and I stress *might*—have been used as part of a summoning symbol for the séance. Apart from the circle and the heaviness, there was not much there, so I headed downstairs.

The second floor was all bedrooms. I went into the daughter's room first which was very neat, almost overly so; I just briefly looked for anything out of the ordinary. There was nothing. The room felt completely peaceful; I always carry some blessed religious paraphernalia with me, so I left a small cross on her bed stand. I then went into what used to be the mother's room. It was as though time had stopped in this room. Everything was exactly as her mother had left it. There was chair by the window and so I sat for a minute just feeling the room. It was just like the owner's daughter's room, very peaceful. I left and continued walking down the hall.

I suddenly felt as though someone was chasing after me; I stopped and a *woosh* of air hit me. I turned around, and as I did, I saw someone leaving the daughter's room. I went in and the cross I had left on the bed stand was broken in two. I nodded my head and thoughi to myself, *Okay, there is something here*. I left the cross where is lay and continued on my way, still feeling as though someone was standing behind me, following my every move.

I went into the owner's room, again looking for anything out of the ordinary, there was a lot of books, but none of a supernatural nature. I decided the basement was my best bet and headed down there. While walking through the house, I went through the living room where my spouse and Jo-anne were talking. When I entered the room, talking stopped and my spouse looked behind me wide-eyed.

"Katie, go and get the things we need; this house needs an exorcism. Now." My spouse talked very calmly and described a man in his late sixties with a button-down-the-front shirt and tweed-like pants. Around him was a black cloud-like form wrapping him at the waist and mouth. The spirit was in pain and trying to gain release but to no avail; the entity would not let go. As my spouse told us what was going on, the owner's face went white; this was her uncle that her mother tried so hard to speak with. And this was the other he told her about.

I went to the car and got my necessities. When I came back in the house, the owner was clinging to my spouse's arm. I figured where I was would be the best place to start. I knew it was still there. I could feel it; the evil of the demon permeated everything around me. I had my spouse take the owner outside while I conducted the exorcism of the house. This entity had no form. It was a shifter. I had seen this a couple of times with other demons. These types have no natural form and change into whatever is most useful to them at the time. I doubted a little that the man was actually the uncle, but knew that if he wasn't part of the evil, the exorcism would not hurt him.

I took out the first of my seals for the control of any evil entity. I wrote down some inscriptions upon it that pertained to the demon. I then threw the seal on the floor and proceeded to stomp on it. Each time I did, I could hear the entity's pain and rage; I continued to thrust my foot onto the seal with all my might. As I did this, I spoke to the demon. I told it of the atrocity it had caused in this house, and that if the demon did not do as I commanded, I would continue to keep the entity in pain. It growled at me. It was trying to distract me, to stop me from hitting the seal. I picked up the seal and held it between my two hands.

"If you do not desist, I will break this seal and you will be forever gone." The growling stopped, "Show yourself to me," I commanded. It did, along with the spirit it had ensnared. I knew then it understood my threat. "Leave this place and you will come to no harm." With that the demon left in a quick whisper of air. I went outside to my spouse and the homeowner. She smiled at me and said, "It's gone. I saw my mother on the porch while we were out here; she told me it's okay now."

We went through the house with white sage to cleanse any residual energy and then sealed all the doors, windows, and other entrances and exits with holy water. I checked in three months later, and the homeowner hasn't had any issues.

It's the Little Things

As you can see, sometimes it is hard to tell if a spirit is a manifestation of a demonic or not, but there is one certain way to tell. Demonic entities will try to appear as friends, family, and sometimes even strangers you don't know, but they will always have a flaw. Sometimes the eyes will be missing, other times the nose will be a little off. Either way, there is always something wrong with their appearance. In this story, the woman had a very strong connection to her mother, and she got a hold of me before things got horribly bad. Spirits will often try to help during these types of situations, much like the mother did with her daughter. But unfortunately, most of the time, they either get taken prisoner or are in fact a manifestation of the demon.

The mother had opened herself and her home to demonic entities years ago—so why did it all start now? Well, actually it hadn't. There had been little things all throughout the daughter's life, but she never put two and two together. I also think that the priest's blessing had helped to keep the entity dormant, until the daughter went rummaging around in the basement, unknowingly reopening the can of worms her mother had tried with the priest's help to close.

These entities are thrifty and know when to stay quite. Years ago, the Uncle tried to warn his sister about the evil in her home, she took heed, and then tried to protect her daughter from it. Spirits in these situations are as much the victims as the living and must be protected as such.

PART II
THE MANIFESTATION

WHAT IS OCCULTISM?

he word *occult* is synonymous in most minds with the word "evil" or "dangerous." Many, when they hear this word, associate it with devil worshippers and demons. But this is not the case; the word *occult* is actually derived from the Latin term *occultus* meaning *hidden or secret*, often used in to convey "knowledge of the hidden." The word in the English language is actually a very broad term, much like the word *pagan* is used to describe any earth-worshipping religion. The word *occult* is used to commonly describe "knowledge of what we don't understand" or "knowledge of the supernatural." You will find many occultists who believe that it is in fact just a deeper understanding of the levels of spiritual truths that surpasses laws of our reality and sciences.

Occult is also used to describe magical or mystical groups also known as orders or organizations and any spiritual or magical texts. The words *arcane* and *esoteric* are commonly thrown around with occult and seem to (nowadays anyway) have the same meaning.

Almost anything that is not accepted as main-stream belief can be considered occult. So, religions such as Judaism, Christianity, Hinduism, Buddhism, and Islam would not be considered occult as the belief systems are widely accepted. Occultists believe that everything in its most basic form is unified, and therefore they aim to become unified with all the rest of the energies the world is made up of. Where a scientist must rely on physically creating static electricity to analyze lightening, the occultist will access the united energy to create or conjure the lightening. As a student of the occult, it is the belief in infinite growth, energy, and ability that allow them to create or manifest phenomena.

Many believe that we have latent abilities and connections to energy that we have not yet even begun to tap into. In this same train of thought, occultists will deal with negative energy, firstly by recognizing it as a part of the universal energy, and secondly, by knowing it can be changed. Many of these practitioners look back to the older texts for direction, although the New Age is becoming more and more mainstream, it is the Old Age that truly guides us.

There are many occult practices that even those who are offended by the term participate in. Here I am going show a list of the most well known (technically) occult practices.

ALCHEMY

An early form of chemistry, that combined metallurgy, astrology, and mysticism.

ANIMISM

The belief that all animals and objects have a soul or spirit.

ASTROLOGY

The occult science of studying the star's placement in relation to an individual.

AUTOMATIC WRITING

The channeling of a spirit through writing.

CANDOMBLE

An Afro-Brazilian religion.

CHANNELING

A controlled spirit possession.

CHIROMANCY

Seeing of the future through analyzing the palm also known as palmistry.

CLAIRAUDIENCE

Literally means "Clear Hearing," the ability to hear spirits, or other entities unable to be seen.

CLAIRVOYANCE

Means "Clear Visibility" the ability to gain information about a person, place or thing without use of the five human senses.

CRYSTALLOMANCY

Crystal gazing, a technique used in which you allow your eyes to rest on crystal ball and see visions of the past, present, or future.

DISCORDIANISM

Modern religion based on the belief that chaos is just as important as order.

DIVINATION

A broad term for different systems of foreseeing the future such as: Tarot cards, tea leaf reading, rune reading, etc.

ECKANKAR

A new religious movement based on the idea that personal spiritual experiences bring a closer relationship to God. According to the Eckankar glossary, the word means "Co-worker with God."

HERMETIC TRADITIONS

A set of philosophical, magical, and religious beliefs based on the teachings of Hermes Trismegistus.

HYDROMANCY

Same as crystal gazing, except you use a pool of water.

INCANTATIONS

Words spoken during a ritual, either a hymn or prayer invoking or in praise of a deity. Also could be a prayer with intent of a specific outcome or happening also known as a spell.

KABBALAH

A school of thought discussing the mystical aspects of Judaism.

MACUMBA

Also known as Quimbanda, is an everyday term used by Brazilians to describe two different types of spirit worship known as Candomble and Umbanda.

MEDIUMS

A person with the ability to contact the dead or other unseen entities.

NECROMANCY
The raising of the dead.

NEO-PAGANISM
A broad term for new religious movements geared toward the revival or pre-Christian beliefs, particularly European such as Celtic, or Italian.

ORDO TEMPLI ORIENTIS
Another fraternal organization; originally supposed to be similar to freemasonry, its objective changed when Aleister Crowley took over and it became based on the Law of Thelema.

OUIJA BOARDS
Also known as a spirit board or a "yes yes board," it is comprised of a board with the alaphabet, numbers, and simple answers written on it. With a planchette or glass, it is used to communicate with spirits or other unseen entities.

PAGANISM
Any earth-worshipping religion, i.e. witchcraft, Native American, etc.

PSYCHOMETRY
The touching of an object and gaining of information through psychic means.

ROSICRUCIANISM
A secret society of mystics built on esoteric truths.

SANTERIA
Afro-Carribean religious tradition.

SEVI LAW, VODUN (VOODOO)
Haitian Voodoo in which they believe that all creation is divine and can be accessed by the practitioners.

SHAMANISM

A large range of traditional beliefs and practices concerning spirits and the spiritual realm. They believe spirits can play an important role in people's lives, that a shaman can work with a spirit for the benefit of self or the community. They also engage in a variety of trance-inducing activities, singing, dancing, drumming, to receive messages from the spirit world.

SPIRITUALISTS

There is a strong belief in God, but they also believe that spirits of the deceased can be accessed through a medium and provide information about the afterlife.

THELEMITE

An adherent of Thelema philosophy based on the idea, "Do what thou wilt."

WITCHCRAFT

An earth-based religion, with the belief of a Mother Goddess and Father God, it represents the duality of nature. Witches recognize that the energy of the universe is the same as their own, and so they are able to work with nature to gain their own ends. A basic principle of the Craft is "An it harm none." It is inspired by old pre-Christian typically European religions; witchcraft is a branch of neo-paganism.

Why are all of these things occult? Well, as I mentioned earlier, occultism is a system which delves into "that which is hidden." Christian religion accepts what God is and how the world works, but does not seek to understand it or believe they are a part of it. Yes, they are God's children, but He is in control of everything. We are His children, and so they do not observe that they are a part of the All. They believe they are a separate entity altogether. Occultism seeks not only to understand what is behind nature and the layers of reality, but also to connect with them.

I have learned much since I started my path. If you look back in the old texts, you will see a lot of astrological, metallurgical, herbal, and magical formulas. For everything on this earth there is an alternate use. Yes, the moon rises at night to give us light, but it also controls the tides, influences the mind, and is a symbolism of the Mysteries of the Universe. There is an herb called mandrake, which is believed to repel demonic entities; mystics believed that the herb was a holy herb. Even in Jewish lore there is mention of King Solomon, who had a ring containing Mandrake and that this ring helped to trap demonic entities. Why am I telling you this? Well, Mandrake is a poisonous herb, that also has many benefits—it is believed to attract love and bring protection to the carrier. That is its magical influence. You see, as I said, in occultism everything has an alternate meaning or representation. It is a matter of looking beyond the obvious.

THE OCCULTISTS

ccultism is mix of fact, formula, and legend. The people involved were real; at some point, they did create formulas with which they contacted the dead, summoned and banished demons, healed the sick, and much more. However, because most of these occultists were larger-than-life characters, some have very elaborate legends that surround them—such as King Solomon, son of King David. Let's take a look at some of the legend, fact, and formulas connected to him.

KING SOLOMON

With a word and a ring, Solomon could pull a demon out of a person's body. Amazing possibilities exist for those who decide to embrace the occult in a positive way. Part of what I do as an Occult Exorcist is to try to erase the stigma that has been placed upon this system of mysticism and magic. The best way to do this is to show you what advances ancient occultists gave to the culture at the time. I am not here to convince you that occultism is the best and only path, but to further expand your horizons.

Let's start with one of the most respected and talked about persons within the field—Solomon, Occultist, Rabbi, and King. Solomon was the son of King David, although not the oldest son. David promised his wife Bathsheba that he would hand the crown to Solomon when it was time. The soon-to-be occultist took over kingship in 967 BCE. The times when David and Solomon ruled were known for peace; Solomon was a distinguished writer, having written three of the books of the Bible, the Song of Solomon, the bulk of the Book of Proverbs, and Ecclesiastes.

> In Gibeon the LORD appeared to Solomon in a dream at night. God said, "Ask something of me and I will give it to you."
> Solomon answered: "You have shown great favor to your servant, my father David, because he behaved faithfully toward you, with justice and an upright heart; and you have continued this great favor toward him, even today, seating a son of his on his throne.
> O LORD, my God, you have made me, your servant, king to succeed my father David; but I am a mere youth, not knowing at all how to act.

" King Solomon passed all the kings of the
earth in riches and wisdom."
—2 *Chron.* ix. 22.

King Solomon sit's upon his throne.

*I serve you in the midst of the people whom you have chosen, a
people so vast that it cannot be numbered or counted.*

*Give your servant, therefore, an understanding heart to judge your
people and to distinguish right from wrong. For who is able to govern
this vast people of yours?"*

The LORD was pleased that Solomon made this request.

*So God said to him: "Because you have asked for this--not for a
long life for yourself, nor for riches, nor for the life of your enemies,
but for understanding so that you may know what is right--*

*I do as you requested. I give you a heart so wise and understanding
that there has never been anyone like you up to now, and after you
there will come no one to equal you.*

~ Kings Chapter 3, verses 5-12

According to rabbinical religious lore, after this conversation with God, the deity not only gave him the understanding, but also bestowed upon him riches, longer life, and a beautiful land, including parts of heaven and all of earth, giving Solomon reign over animals, spirits, and demons.

There is also another interesting story that speaks of the ring King Solomon wore. Supposedly, there was a boy who the king favored who was being attacked by a demon. Solomon, being distraught over this, went to his temple and prayed. There, the Archangel Michael came down from Heaven and bestowed upon him a ring which would later be considered the Seal of Solomon. It was believed to have been made of either brass or iron with four jewels embedded into it, along with the inscription of the name of God. It gave him the power over the elements, the ability to speak with animals, and to trap demons into jars, vessels, and even statues.

There is much question around the validity of this tale, however, there may be hope yet! It is believed that Alexander the Great came into possession of the ring, and this is what aided him in his near conquering of the world. It is said that when he died, he was laid in a tent with all sides of the cloth structure pulled up so that his army would be able to see him one last time. There was script stating that the ring still rested upon Alexander's finger at this time, although it is believed Ptolemy actually stole the body of Alexander as it traveled back to Macedon, and the ring along with it. After this point, there is no more information about the ring resurfacing.

S. Liddell MacGregor Mathers was an author, occult scholar, and helped initiate the revival of the occult in the late 1800s. He, along with two others, founded The Hermetic Order of the Golden Dawn. It seemed that S.L. Mathers was in fact a master linguist with knowledge of a wide variety of both living and dead languages. He put himself to the test of translating many archaic works to make them available to those who were not as highly educated and spoke only

The Sixth Pentacle of Mars from The Key Of Solomon the King (Clavicula Salomonis) by S.L. Mathers.

English. He published a variety of works on King Solomon's occult texts, which included magical seals, with translations of such books like: *The Red Dragon*, also known as the *Grand Grimoire*, *The Lesser Keys of Solomon*, and *The Book of the Sacred Magic of Abramelin the Mage.*

Although his work at the time was viewed as incomplete or not up to par by others within the community, such as A.E. Waite, it has stood the test of time, and his texts have become a huge resource for both old initiates and budding occultists.

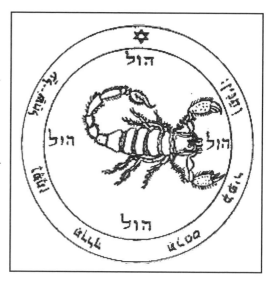

The Fifth Pentacle of Mars from The Key Of Solomon the King (Clavicula Salomonis) by S.L. Mathers.

JOHANN WEYER

This person is a large influence in my life. Taught by one of the most well-known occultists, Henry Cornelius Agrippa, Weyer was not just a practitioner of magical arts, but a demonologist and a pioneer in medicine and psychiatry. Johann was born in 1515 in Grave, Netherlands. He attended Latin schools until the age of fourteen when he became a live-in student of the great Henry Agrippa. Later, the duo left Antwerp and, in 1533, Agrippa completed a work on demons, then died in 1535.

Left without his teacher, Weyer went on to study medicine in Paris. After spending a short time as a physician in his home town, he was given the office of town physician in Arnhem, where he was asked for his input of cases of witchcraft due to his position. In 1550, Weyer moved on to Cleves where he was appointed Court Physician to a Duke William. It was while there that he created a text entitled, *"De Praestigiis Daemonum et Incantationibus ac Venificiis"* or *"On the Illusions of the Demons and on Spells and Poisons."* It was written in response to the *Malleus Maleficarum* or Witch Hunter's Handbook, the *Praestigiis Daemonum*, criticizing both the book and the witch trials. Weyer was believed to be the first person to have used the term "mental illness" during the witch trials. He discussed this in his book, *Deceptions of Demons*, in 1583, giving examples such as:

> *"About 40 people at Casale in Western Lombardy smeared the bolts of the town gates with an ointment to spread the plague. Those who touched the gates were infected and many died. The heirs of the dead and diseased had actually paid people at Casale to smear the gates in order to obtain their inheritances more quickly."*
> ~ From Deceptions of Demons, Johann Weyer, 1583

He worked towards getting the authority taken away from local government and given to physicians and the church so that they may take care of these women. His third book, *Pseudomonarchia Daemonum* (The False Kingdom of Demons) is a catalogue of demonic entities and how to raise or receive things from them. Weyer believed that demons had power, and that they could appear before a person who called them, that they could also cast illusions, but that the Church gave the demonic entities too much credit. (He mentioned this in *Praestigiis Daemonum*.)

When discussing the raising of demons in conjunction with illusions, he would refer to magicians, explaining the they used the Devil's power to do it. However, when pressed about the same issues surrounding witches, he claimed they were just mentally ill.

In *Psuedomonarchia Daemonum*, Weyer gives descriptions and instructions for times, dates, and incantations to conjure each demon in the name of God. These sacred words were used not to create impressive illusions (such as riches or women), but to force the entity to do what the summoner wanted. He also included a few tips on dealing with demons who did not want to work with the conjurer or would not give an honest answer.

Weyer was an advocate for the abolishment of the witch trials altogether, feeling it unnecessary. Being an occultist himself, this was very thin ice for him to tread upon, because back then it did not take much to be accused of being a consort to the devil.

When writing of the demons in *Psuedomonarchia Daemonum*, he loosely refers to the entities as "spirits" and seems to carefully use the word exorcist. One may assume from his texts that he knew much about the subject. However, back then, I don't believe they made the connection between his studies and his practices. Weyer was an inspiration to many occultists, and *Psuedomonarchia Daemonum* became such a hit that there were several editions printed in Latin. Then Reginald Scot made the first translation into English and several more editions were printed from there.

HEINRICH CORNELIUS AGRIPPA

Agrippa was a magician, alchemist, astrologer, and occult author. Born in 1486 in Germany, he studied under Johannes Trithemius Abbot of Spanheim, near Würzburg in 1510, where he created what would eventually be his masterpiece, *De occulta philosophia libri tres* (The book of Occult Philosophy). Trithemius approved of the work but suggested that it not be published. Agrippa took his teacher's advice, continuing to reformat and revise the book over the next twenty years. Agrippa spent the bulk of his life in travel, from Germany, to Italy and France, he held highly respected positions such as theologian, physician, and was a soldier. While in the service of Maximilian I, Agrippa continued his studies of the occult. Throughout his life, he was always attracting scandal or backlash of some sort—typically, for his theological views, not position or views in the occult.

He was never openly accused of heresy, but behind closed doors people threw the word around in connection with him. There is no proof that Agrippa was ever accused of heresy in connection with the occult and magical interests he had. However, it did cause him to lose several positions of authority. He finally printed his *De occulta philosophia libri tres* in 1533, but before the book was even been printed, it was denounced as heresy by the Dominican Inquisitor Conrad Köllin of Ulm. The Occult Philosophy became three books actually, and became influential to many of the occultists after him, such as John Dee and Giordano Bruni (a priest and occultist). In it he defends magicians saying,

> *"I do not doubt but the Title of our book of* Occult Philosophy, *or of Magick, may by the rarity of it allure many to read it, amongst which, some of a crasie [languid, feeble] judgement, and some that are perverse will come to hear what I can say, who, by their rash ignorance may take the name of Magick in the worse sense, and though scarce having seen the title, cry out that I teach forbidden Arts, sow the seed of Heresies, offend pious ears, and scandalize excellent wits; that I am a sorcerer, and superstitious and divellish [devilish], who indeed am a Magician: to whom I answer, that a Magician doth not amongst learned men signifie a sorcerer, or one that is superstitious or divellish [devilish]; but a wise man, a priest, a prophet; and that the Sybils were Magicianesses, and therefore prophecyed most cleerly of Christ; and that Magicians, as wise men…"*
>
> ~ De occulta philosophia libri tres (*Occult Philosophy* Book 1 Natural Magic— - Agrippa to the Reader)

In 1559, there mysteriously appeared a fourth book of *Occult Philosophy* referred to as "Of Magickal Ceremonies" that was supposedly written by Agrippa, but this claim appears spurious, and is not his work at all.

Agrippa, also know for theological studies, wrote several books on his work including, *Declamatio de nobilitate et praecellentia foeminei sexus*. Declamation on the Nobility and Preeminence of the Female Sex in 1529. Originally written in Latin, it was published in English in 1670, and was one of the first texts with a feminist view.

All in all, Agrippa was a controversial, but highly respected figure in his community both for this theology, occult works, and his work as a physician.

ALPHONSE LOUIS CONSTANT

The occultist who would come to be known as Eliphas Levi was born in 1810 under the name of Alphonse Louis Constant. The son of a shoemaker, his father wanted his only son to have a good education, but knew he could not afford to finance his studies, and so he sent his offspring to seminary to be educated and trained as a priest. Before he finished his schooling, Alphonse fell deeply in love and left before his ordination. After this, he wrote a couple of religious articles, then two radical texts— one called the "Gospel of the People" in 1840 and another called "The Testament of Liberty," this written in what was called the Year of Revolution in 1848. At this time, there was a lot of upheaval within the government and community. Alexis de Tocqueville, a French political thinker and historian, published this comment in his text called "Recollections:"

"Society was cut in two: those who had nothing united in common envy, and those who had anything united in common terror."

Because of Alphonse's left wing views regarding

Eliphas Levi, creator of the Baphomet.

the government reformation, he unfortunately was put into prison twice, both for short amounts of time.

Constant had been introduced to occultism while in seminary and, after leaving, met a couple named Ganneau. The man believed he was a reincarnation of Louis XVII and his wife was originally Marie Antoinette. After hearing many of their magical exploits, Alphonse became their student. Soon after, he began to use the name Eliphas Levi, what he believed to be a Hebrew translation of his first and middle names. While visiting with a friend of his, Edward Bulwer-Lytton, who had always had an interest in Rosicrucianism and was president of a minor Rosicrucian Order, Levi first began thinking of writing a magical treatise.

Levi made his living teaching the occult and writing for various journals. His first foray into necromancy occurred in 1854, where a woman claiming to be an experienced magician asked him to summon the spirit of a great Magus named Apollonius of Tyana. After two weeks of a strict diet, fasting, and meditation, where he imagined conversations with the sorcerer, Levi felt ready to begin the ritual.

He entered his sacred chamber with tools at the ready; he had many mirrors within his space and two bowls set upon a table where he lit fires. With everything prepared, he began the incantations for conjuration which lasted twelve hours. The room became colder the more he progressed with the ritual, and then the floor began to shake beneath him. Finally, an apparition appeared in one of the mirrors and he demanded that it present itself in front him—which it did, touching the tip of Levi's ritual sword, causing the arm to go limp and for him to pass out. Levi claimed that for days afterward the arm was sore.

Levi was uncertain as to whether, in this particular instance, he truly summoned the spirit of the Magus, but claimed later he successfully did so many times.

During the year 1855, Levi came out with his first bit of work called *Dogme et Rituel de la Haute Magie* or The Dogma and Ritual of High Magic, which later would be translated into English by Arthur Edward Waite under the title "Transcendental Magic, its Doctrine and Ritual." There is a famous line in the beginning of this book which some say is an essential to read. It goes as follows:

> *"Behind the veil of all the hieratic and mystical allegories of ancient doctrines, behind the darkness and strange ordeals of all initiations, under the seal of all sacred writings, in the ruins of Nineveh or Thebes, on the crumbling stones of old temples and on the blackened visage of the Assyrian or Egyptian sphinx, in the monstrous or marvelous*

paintings which interpret to the faithful of India the inspired pages of the Vedas, in the cryptic emblems of our old books on alchemy, in the ceremonies practiced at reception by all secret societies, there are found indications of a doctrine which is everywhere the same and everywhere carefully concealed."

Around the year 1861, Levi had publish what seemed to be a companion to his first called *La Clef des Grands Mysteres* (The Key to the Great Mysteries). There are many works written by Levi, such as *Fables et Symboles*, (Stories and Images in 1862), *La Science des Esprits* (The Science of Spirits in 1865), and *Le Grand Arcane, ou l'Occultisme Devoile* (The Great Secret, or Occultism Unveiled 1868).

While well known for his occult writings, there is one thing Levi is even more famous for—his creation of the Baphomet, which he claimed was a symbol of the absolute in all its forms. This depiction is supposedly the deity that the Knights Templar worshipped. It is believed by some to be inspired by a gargoyle which stands upon one of the buildings of the Knights Templar called the Commandry of Saint Bris le Vineux.

The depiction of the goat does look foreboding, but if one looks past the surface, you can see that it symbolizes the polarities and dual nature of all. The light moon and the dark moon, it combines the masculine and feminine in the arms, breasts, and phallus. In the hands, one points up while the other down, almost as if in symbol showing the now familiar creed of many of today's Hermetic traditions, "As Above, So Below." The symbol also contains texts "Solve" which is written on the right arm and "Coagula" on the left. (Solve meaning solution and coagula mean coagulation.) Both things familiar to Levi as alchemical studies, he not only practiced, but wrote about them. He explains it best with this quote:

"Moreover, the sign of occultism is made with both hands, pointing upward to the white moon of Chesed, and downward to the black moon of Geburah. This sign expresses the perfect concord between mercy and justice. One of the arms is feminine and other masculine, as in the Androgyne of Khunrath, whose attributes we have combined with those of our goat, since they are one and the same symbol. The torch of intelligence burning between the horns is the magical light of universal equilibrium; it is also the type of soul exalted above matter, as the flame cleaves to the torch. The monstrous head of the animal expresses horror of sin, for which the material agent, alone responsible, must alone and for ever bear the penalty, because the soul is impassible in its nature and can suffer only by materialising. The caduceus, which replaces the generative organ, represents eternal life; the scale-covered belly tyifies

Levi's Baphomet.

water; the circle above it is the atmosphere; the feathers still higher up signify the volatile; lastly, humanity is depicted by the two breasts and the androgyne arms of this sphinx of the occult sciences"

~ Transcendental Magic written by Levi translated by
A.E. Waite

Levi also believed the name Baphomet to have special meaning, if written backwards it spells:

TEM OHP AB

He believed these short words to be the abbreviated Latin representing the phrase "Templi omnivm hominum pacis abbas," the translation being, "The Father Of The Temple Of Peace Of All Men," a direct reference to King Solomon's Temple which he believed to have been constructed specifically to help bring peace to all of humanity.

A.E. Waite believed so much in Levi's Baphomet that he in fact included the image into the Devil card of his Rider-Waite tarot deck. Levi did include extensive work with tarot as part of his studies and system of magic and, therefore, I believe that the deck is an awesome way to honor him.

Levi's magical works and writing influence occultism even in today's society. These magical works made a huge impact on Hermetic Order of The Golden Dawn. He is also known for inspiring the occultist, Aleister Crowley, who was born the same year that Levi died in 1875. Crowley believed he was a reincarnation of Eliphas Levi and tried to continue what he believed was Levi's work.

APOLLONIUS OF TYANA

Apollonius was born at Tyana in Asia Minor in 40 AD. He earned his schooling in Tarsus and then at the Temple of Aesculapius, where at the young age of sixteen, he became a follower of Pythagoras. Many mysteries surround this historical figure who is often regarded as a modern Christ. He traveled from town to town preaching his beliefs and performing miracles. He was active in Italy, Spain, Ethiopia, and traveled as far as Mesopotamia, Arabia, and India.

Along the way, a scribe joined him named Philostratus II. He was asked by Empress Julia Domna, and completed his work on Apollonius after the Empress's death. So the magician wandered the continents making miracles, preaching, and casting predictions. In one case, he was visiting the city of Ephesus where he tried to warn the people of a horrible plague that would wipe out the city. No one paid this preacher any attention, even after the sickness that was predicted started to happen.

But after a little while, they began to remember the man that tried to tell them of the pestilence on its way. They asked him what they could do to stop the sickness and Apollonius calmly told them of a beggar who wandered the streets of Ephesus, that the homeless man must be stoned to death. The residents were wary of performing such a task, but Apollonius insisted that this was the only way to rid oneself of the plague. So finally they agreed. After the stoning took place, the people removed the rubble and where once the beggar laid, dead and cold, a black dog now took the wretch's place. Apollonius pronounced that this animal was the cause of the pestilence which infected the city.

Now, as I said previously, Apollonius was a Pythagorean and did not approve of animal sacrifice, and ate a strict vegetarian diet. He also believed that God could not be summoned through prayer and animal sacrifice. There is actually a fragment of text (believed to be authentic) of Apollonius which describes his belief on sacrifice:

> *"that God, who is the most beautiful being, cannot be influenced by prayers or sacrifices and has no wish to be worshipped by humans, but can be reached by a spiritual procedure involving nous, because he himself is pure nous and nous is also the greatest faculty of mankind."*
>
> ~Dzielska p. 139-141

Nous is the philosophical term for mind or intellect. Pythagoras was a mystic who used a system of mathematics to obtain wisdom and Apollonius carried on this same belief that the mind is what God would react to—not sacrifice or prayers. Many have found this to be an almost universal truth; if you think on something you want enough, it will come to you. Apollonius was also believed to be a psychic; he showed his abilities when Emperor Domitian was murdered in 96 A.D. in Rome. At the time the magician was in Ephesus, he claimed to have witnessed the event in a vision on the exact day and hour of the murder. He told those around him of what he had seen.

When Apollonius traveled to Rome, the consular there believed his daughter to be dead (although no one, even Philostratus, knew whether she was dead of just appeared to be), and so Apollonius spent time with the body of the girl which resulted in her returning to life.

Apollonius was a known and highly-regarded figure in the medieval Islamic world and gained notoriety and the name "Lord of Talismans." He often appears in Islamic literature as Balīnūs; Arabic occultists often related stories of the magician's talisman makings. They believed he had mastered the art of alchemy and was a wealth of hermetic knowledge. There were many occult texts that were published under his name in the Islamic Middle Ages, mostly concerning his work with seals, sigils, amulets and talismans. Here are some of the texts that were written under his name:

* *The Book of Causes*
* *Treatise on the influence of the spiritual beings on the composite things*
* *Great introduction to the treatise on the talismans*
* *Great book of* Balīnūs' *talismans*
* *Book of the sage Albus*

In the Tablet of Wisdom written by Bahá'u'lláh, the founder of the Bahá'í Faith, he mentions Balīnūs with great respect and reverence saying:

> *"This man hath said: `I am Bálinus, the wise one, the performer of wonders, the producer of talismans.' He surpassed everyone else in the diffusion of arts and sciences and soared unto the loftiest heights of humility and supplication."*
>
> ~Tablet of Wisdom

In respect to Apollonius' talismans, later after his death, they began to appear in several cities within the Roman Empire. They were meant to protect these towns from various "evils," such as sickness and poverty. During this time, Christians were attempting to convert many of the pagans and so it was with some difficulty they tried to get these symbols removed, claiming they were the work of demons. Many claimed that these talismans would do no harm and were actually beneficial. No matter what each side believed, there was never any mention that the seals failed in their respective duties.

Apollonius was also known for the expelling of demons. Philostratus, his constant biographer, did his best to write everything he could on the miracle worker. There are a couple of texts within the eight books that document Apollonius' life that detail accounts of exorcisms which the magician performed. Here are a couple of those stories.

> *"As (Apollonius) was discussing libations, there was a youth nearby who had such a name for luxury and vulgarity that by then there were even street songs about him. His homeland was Corcyra and he was descended from Alcinus, Odysseus' Phaecian host.*

Apollonius was speaking about libations and told them not to drink from this cup but to keep it untouched and unused for the gods. But when he told them also to put handles on the cup and (in the libation) to pour it over these—since men are less apt to drink (there)—the youth drowned out his word with loud and course laughter. Looking up at him, (Apollonius) said:

"These insults are not from you but from the demon who drives you without your knowing it." The youth was in fact demon-possessed, for he laughed at things that no one else did. And then he would change to weeping without having any reason to. And he would talk and sing to himself. Now, the people thought that it was the unruliness of youth that led him to do these things. But it was the demon acting. And he seemed to be drunk only because he was then drinking. Apollonius stared at him; and the phantom started uttering sounds of fear and rage, like those who are burnt and tortured. And the phantom promised to leave the youth alone and never take possession of people again. But speaking with anger like a master to a slave who is unstable, mischievous, shameless, and so forth, (Apollonius) ordered him to depart and to provide proof (that he had done so). (The demon) said: "I will knock down that statue," pointing to one of those on the royal porch. When the statue first shook and then fell, there was more commotion and applause at the marvel than anyone could write about. But the youth just rubbed his eyes, as if he was waking up and saw the sun's rays. And he won the attention over everyone who turned to him. For he no longer seemed vulgar, nor did he cast his eyes wildly about. But he returned to his natural self, as if he had been medicated. And he threw away the gowns and dresses of Sybarites and developed a love for a rough shirt and cloak and modeled his behavior on that of Apollonius."

~ Philostratus, Life of Apollonius of Tyana 4.20

"In the middle of these sayings, the messenger arrived with Indians begging the sages for help. He presented a woman pleading for her child. She said he was sixteen years old; and for two years he had a demon. The demon's behavior was irony and lying. One of the sages asked why she said this. She said: "This child is very good looking, so the demon is in love. He doesn't let him have a mind to go either to school or archery practice or even to stay home. He drives him out to deserted spots. The boy no longer even has his own voice. His speech is deep and hollow like that of adult males. And he stares with someone else's eyes rather than his own. And I weep and claw my face and try to call my son back any way I can. But he does not know me. When I planned my trip here—this was planned a year ago—the demon

revealed himself by using the child as his persona. He told me he is the phantom of a man who died in battle long ago. He died loving his wife. But three days after his death his wife insulted his bed by marrying again. He came to loathe the love of women and redirected it to this child. If I agreed not to denounce him before you, he promised me he will give my son much fortune and good. For these things I endured this for awhile. But he has already deceived me for a long time. And he has complete control of my house, plotting nothing fair or true."
(Apollonius) *the sage asked again if the child were nearby.*

But she said: "No. I tried many things to make him come. But the demon threatens to jump off cliffs and into pits and to kill my son, if I bring him here for trial."

The sage said:"Courage! he will not kill him when he reads this."

And he took a letter from his shirt and give it to this woman. Now the letter was addressed to the phantom and contained threats and other terrifying things."
~Philostratus, Life of Apollonius of Tyana 3.38

Apollonius was both a sage, and mystic, but he was also a great philosopher. He traveled to Rome during the time of Nero, who was a horrible Emperor, more concerned with his music and private life than his country. However, he was beloved by the lower classes, but feared by those closest to him. In the beginning of his reign, he committed matricide, killing his mother, Agrippina; his wife died not long after. In the year 64, having felt abandoned, Nero sunk totally into his private life, not even wanting to deal with his responsibilities and so Tigellinus (a terrible and cruel man) became the foremost advisor to Nero, and basically had free reign. Nero was worshipped like a god among his people, even though he committed such horrendous crimes as the burning of Rome, torture, and barbarity against the Christians. Now you may wonder what Nero had to do with Apollonius; well it just so happened that, one day, the magician was nearby. Here is what his biographer wrote of the time:

"An epidemic which the doctors call influenza has Rome. It stirred up coughing fits and speakers' voice became bad. Now emples were full of people petitioning the gods because Nero had a sore throat and was suffering with a husky voice. Apollonius let out (a comment) on the insanity of the crowd, but criticized no one. Rather he even calmed Menippus, who was irritated by such things, and cautioned him: "Excuse the gods, if they are pleased to be mimicked by clowns."

When this saying was reported to Tigellinus [the chief of Nero's secret police], he sent agents to put (Apollonius) in prison, since he was charged with irreverence to Nero. A prosecutor who had already done away with many and a veteran of such Olympiads was appointed for him. In his hands he had a certain writ on which the charge had been written. And he held it up to the man, like a sword, and said it was sharp enough to ruin him. But when Tigellinus unrolled the writ, he did not find a trace of writing on it. He was confronted by a blank book. So he thought he was dealing with a demon. It is said that later Domitian also felt this way about (Apollonius). Then taking Apollonius, (Tigellinus) entered a secret court in which the officer in question passed judgment on major cases in private. When he had made everyone (else) leave, he interrogated (Apollonius), asking who he might be. Apollonius mentioned his father and his homeland, and explained why he preoccupied himself with wisdom. He said he practiced it to know the gods and to understand the (lot) of humans. For it is harder to know another than to know oneself. (Tigellinus) said: "How do you rebuff demons and the appearance of phantoms, Apollonius?" (Apollonius) replied: "Like murderers and irreverent humans."

He said this as an insult to Tigellinus, who was Nero's teacher in every cruelty and brutality... (Tigellinus) said: "Why aren"t you afraid of Nero?" (Apollonius) replied: "Because the God who lets him seeming frightening also made me to be unafraid." (Tigellinus) said: "What is your opinion of Nero?" (Apollonius) replied:

"Higher than yours. For you hold him worthy to sing, but I (hold) him worthy of silence." Shocked by this, Tigellinus said: "You may go. But you must post a bond for your body."

Apollonius said: "And what will be the bond for a body which no one will bind?"

To Tigellinus, these things seemed to be demonic and beyond human (wit); and since he was too cautious to match wits with a god, he said:

"Go where you want. For you are too powerful to be ruled by me."
~Philostratus, Life of Apollonius of Tyana 4.44

Nero ended up committing assisted suicide near the end of his reign and was "erased" from most art containing his image. Paintings were re-painted to make it look like someone else; this is not uncommon to do within the Roman Empire when a disgraceful Emperor dies. However, no matter how horrible Nero may have been, it is my belief that he never wanted the position in the first place—he was always in love with his music, never his country.

Apollonius, a magician, sage, philosopher, and miracle worker, lived long past the average age into his 100s. It is believed he was able to retain his youthfulness because of a trip to India he made in which he met a man who made seven rings, each with magical abilities. The elder taught Apollonius how to make these rings, and it is said that these objects are what allowed him to live past his prime. It is a mystery as to how Apollonius actually died; some say that he fell out of favor with the Emperor Severus and that the patriarch cut off the magician's hair to take away his power, and yet others say that he ascended to heaven. After his death, many temples were erected in his honor, and even now, some believe that he was what the Christian Jesus was originally based.

WORKING WITH MAGICAL SEALS AND SIGILS

igils are pictures and symbols that represent certain spiritual beings; they can also be a collection of words and symbols brought together for a specific intent, such as, healing the sick, trapping a demon, protection, money, etc. The sigil is just the art, not what the design is drawn upon; sigils can be used anywhere. Many of the talismans we wear today, are sigils. The holy cross could technically be considered a sigil as it is believed to bring protection and keep the spiritual entity Jesus close by. Your name is your sigil; if someone calls it, you answer.

The root of this word is Latin coming from the word *sigillum*, meaning little seal of signet. Up until just a few centuries ago, we used sigils to identify ourselves and our places of birth. Many know of how kings had signet rings which they pressed into wax to seal their papers. This would be considered the king's sigil. In occultism, much like in Catholicism, if you have the name, then you can control the entity, as the name signifies the identity and abilities of the entity.

The word *sigil* is often used interchangeably with seal and that is not so. They are not the same thing. A sigil would be just the graphic representation of the entity or intention, whereas the seal is much more than that. It contains alchemical, astrological, and other occult symbols that represent the entity and its abilities. Sometime the seal will have the entities, or Gods' names in either Greek, Hebrew, or Latin.

Typically, a seal is in a circular shape with another inner circle in the innermost circle which would be the symbol of the entity or intent; in the ring between the two circles would be the name of the spirit or more symbology to empower the seal.

When it comes to magic with entities, there are several terms that seem to often become confused. Firstly, is the seal or sigil which we just explained. Then there is the signature, which is just that, a signature. Yes, spirits or entities will write often—it is in an archaic alphabet and also obscured by the entity, inverting the letters or writing them backwards and sometimes even signing them upside down. It is not possible to typically read the signature of a spirit, as they are written in a line similar to how we would sign ours. As I said earlier, their signatures are often so distorted that you never know which entity is really being represented. But what I also said before, you know the name; you have the power. They don't give it up willingly.

The reason I am talking about signatures, which are also called characters, is because often you will hear someone refer to a seal or sigil as a spirit's or entity's written name. But it also makes sense, considering that not long ago we were a widely illiterate people who made a "mark" in order to sign a document. That is why the term signature still carries with it the underlying meaning of a seal. As much as, back then, we had our marks, so we gave these sigils to the entitys to better understand and work with them.

The word *sign* is also often used to describe all of the terms we just talked about, but it actually refers to any occult or obscure symbol—such as the alchemical symbols would be considered signs. A glyph, short for the term hieroglyph, is also a pictorial representation of a letter; this is used mainly in terms of astrology. So the II of Gemini would be called a glyph. Both Egyptians and Chinese use this method of communication.

Amulets and talismans can be inscribed with sigils, however, if there is not material body, then they do not exist, where as the sigil does exist, as it is something that can be meditated upon and recalled at will. Now what is the difference between an amulet and a talisman? Well, a big one. Amulets are typically worn where as talismans are carried. So if you think about a kings ring and the sigil it carries would be considered an amulet, but a police officer's badge, which could be construed as a symbol of protection would be considered a talisman as it is carried on the body, not worn.

Sigils are still commonly used in the Kabbalah to summon Gods or angels. Medieval occultists used these sigils for everything from Gods to demons, they also believed in lower spirits which were used to gain more selfish ends, such as finding treasure, finding favor with women, winning wars, etc. When the entity was summoned, having control was easy if you had their sigil, any harm inflicted upon the sigil would have the same effect upon the entity itself; much like with a voodoo doll, the occultist would pierce the sigil with a pin, place it inside a Bible, bury it, bind it, or hold it over open flames. Often, just the occultist mentioning that he/she would destroy the sigil compelled the demon to do whatever the person wanted. In this way, the magician showed how he/she had complete control over the entity and the spirit would bend to the magician's will in order to escape unscathed.

Sigils and seals can be used in many different ways; through meditation you can focus on the pictograph imbuing it with what you wish to achieve. Ultimately, I like to have mine written down; in the old days, virgin parchment was the cream of the crop, but now it is rather hard to get and incredibly expensive. Virgin parchment is hard to burn or destroy, so if you can get your hands on it, I suggest just getting a sheet or two they can be used to make up to sixteen seals or sigils. If you cannot get that but wish to still have an old world feel about it you can get various types of parchment paper anywhere. I suggest getting the thicker parchment, as it doesn't split or bend as easily. You can also engrave your symbols into metals, glass, or stones.

Stones are a wonderful tool when doing sigil work; think of Runes that we use today as a divination system. To the early Germanic tribes, they were also sigils; the arrow depicted strength and is a mark of the warrior. Today, you can find these pretty much anywhere. But when working with a sigil, if you intend for it to be used to a specific end, you need to find a stone that works with it accordingly. Such as, bringing peace to a loved one, you would want to find a stone known for peace, such as Rose Quartz. You can then engrave or paint the stone with the sigil, charge the whole thing with your intent to help this loved one attain a peaceful state of living, and give it to them to carry on them or leave in the house.

Seals and sigils can also be put on cloth, wood, inscribed in clay and leathers. In our technological age, seals are now appearing in all forms on the Internet making it easier for those interested in the art to learn how.

The great thing about seals is they are inherently a neutral tool that can be easily adapted to any situation, entity, or religion. My favorites are Solomon Seals, completely adaptable, and they work really well. I like to use parts of the Solomon seals and then add some of my own work to it, I am not suggesting you go out and take apart a seal and put it back together. You need to be aware that some seals have specific symbols and words you need to keep grouped together in order for them to work. This type of magic could occupy a book in itself (it has, and there are many of them out there), but here I am just trying to give you a basic idea of their workings.

There are many occult texts or Grimoires containing seals and sigils that can be used. The most well known are the Lesser Key of Solomon, the Goetia, sixten and seventh Book of Moses, and the Grand Grimoire is another of these great literatures containing seals and sigils. Many of the pictographs you will find in these books have glyphs, magical writings, and some form of geometry or drawing inside of them. It is important to understand that while these symbols are very old, they are in fact useless unless charged for their purpose. Most of the time, the rituals to imbue them are very outlandish and complex, so it is best to start simple and work your way up.

MAKE YOUR OWN:

To make your own personal sigil is relatively easy. This is something you can use to create a seal of empowerment, bring business, etc. This would be the base for your seal.

Think of a seal this way:

Inside the inner circle is the "who." Who is this going to be affecting/summoning?

Outside the circle is the "how." How is this going to effect/bind/ bring something?

So, to make your own personal sigil you would use your name (either magical or the name you were born with). If you have a first, middle, and last, you would use the first letter of each name to make a very basic sigil. We will use the name Alice Kerry Montgomery just for this purpose.

So the letters you would use would be:

A K M

Okay, next you would arrange these letters into a sigil by finding a means to essentially squish them together. Here are a few ways to do it (see Figure 2.1-2):

Now we can pretty them up by adding color or curlicues (see Figure 2.3).

Figure 2.1.

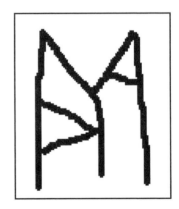

Figure 2.2.

Those details don't mean anything; they are more to hide what the sigil actually is. But you may feel free to add any religious elements or important things into your sigil—it is supposed to embody you. Just remember to keep it simple.

Alright, so let's figure that Alice wants to bring money to her. To make a simple seal (you can use both ancient and modern symbology; there are no restrictions), you would place the symbols in between the sigil's two circles (see Figure 2.4).

In the four directions, we have placed symbols; the words form the in-between spaces. At the top is the money symbol, because that is what Alice wants most. But remember, the outer ring is the "how." The Gemini symbol which comes next represents Alice again; she is a Gemini. It is also a sign of communication which

Figure 2.3.

is another reason she has the symbol there. Next, is the planetary sign for Jupiter and then the Sun, both planets of success. Jupiter also brings generosity and joy to life, the sun brings with it (aside from success), glory and recognition. So those make up the symbols. But what of the words? These words are written in Latin. When making your seal, you can easily look up a Hebrew or Latin translator right on the Internet or even write your intent in English. I suggest trying it in one of the other two languages though (Hebrew or Latin) just in case someone gets a hold of your seal. You may not want them knowing what you are attempting to do.

Figure 2.4.

What Alice wrote was:

"Bring me money, Bring me business success."

This translated into:

"Addo mihi Viaticus Addo Mihi Res prosperitas"

...which we then evenly distributed among the seal. Now we must charge the seal by burning incense and myrrh. You fill a cup or bowl with blessed salt and let the seal sit in it for a couple of minutes, then run the seal through the smoke of the frankincense and myrrh while focusing your intent on it, and calling for your Deities to bless it. This is the easiest way to bless and charge your seals.

I want to make one important thing very clear: A seal is not a magic circle! Magical circles are entirely different, and if you attempt to use a seal as a circle, it will not work towards your goal. Although, say in our example, Alice decided to draw the seal onto the floor at work hidden under a rug. It may bring more business to her.

However magical circles are used strictly for containment, protection during ritual and summoning. A magical circle can also be known as a pentacle; these diagrams typically have some ritual function and are often drawn on the floor. Often the conjurer will stand inside a pentacle while summoning a demonic entity to another circle outside of the pentacle—ensuring no harm is done to the conjurer.

Most of the sigil writing you will find is based in Kabbalah, much like Solomon's pentacles and seals. It is not uncommon to see the letters "YHWH" in a seal or "TETRAGRAMMATON" or "ALPHA" and "OMEGA". Tetragrammaton is specifically speaking of YHWH, "tetra" meaning four and "gramma" meaning letter. YHWH pronounced as *Adomai* is the sacred name of god. Here is the funny thing about this name YHWH—it is a radical of H-W-H, which in the middle east meant *being, life, or women* and was interchangeable depending on the situation. In Latin, the letters become E-V-E or *Eve* so we can then deduce that what the Tetragrammaton is truly referring to is Eve the Mother of All Things. To go a little further, the Gnostic Gospels also stated their belief in the Mother Goddess archetype and they had a story that talked about how the Mother had a Son and He stole her powers and created the world. The Gnostics believed that this Son was in fact who the Christians worshipped, not the real Mother who created the world. There is a second version of the Tetragrammaton also known as EHYH which refers to Hayya, one of Eve's many names; this is strictly speaking about the Goddess and her connection to women in childbirth.

Alpha and Omega is based on the first and last letters of the Greek alphabet; it is the beginning of all things and the end of all things. Revelation 1:8 in the King James Version of the Bible states:

"I am Alpha and Omega, the first and the last."

Christians believe this to mean that God was there at the beginning of time and will be at the end; others in the faith believe it to mean that Jesus was part of the trinity before coming to earth and continues to be after. In Judaism, there is a well religious maxim that says:

"The seal of God is Emet"

...which in Hebrew means, truth and is taken from the first, middle, and last letters of the alphabet. So that is Josephus defined God as "the beginning, middle and end of all things."

The thing you need to be most wary of when creating seals is your state of mind during the creation; do not attempt any type of magic when depressed, or in a melancholy state. You have to remember these seals rely on your energy to work and what you send out there will be returned. So if in fact you create a seal for happiness while depressed, you may in fact make your depression worse, no matter what type of symbology is on the seal. Be cautious, and please be smart—do not attempt any type of summoning unless you are an adept and properly trained.

SUMMONING DEMONS

ccultism teaches that there are many layers to reality, that there are many parallel worlds and alternate universes with their own species and inhabitants. It also teaches us to be wary of which we invite to our time, like a big gateway; words in a book or using a Ouija unprotected can unknowingly invite these entities. These beings will feast upon you, using you to their benefit.

The idea of summoning demons go back to the time of King Solomon and his legends; most of the books you will find today claim to be a derivative of King Solomon's invocations, seals, and sigils. Supposedly, Solomon used a ring he created to command demons to build his temple where all could worship. There is a door of the temple that, according to lore, was built by Asmodeus. Throughout time, there have been stories of selling one's soul to the devil, conjuring demons, and so forth. We are going to talk a little bit about that, but lets start with one of the most infamous of legends.

"E'en hell hath it's peculiar laws"

~ *Faust*, **Johann Wolfgang van Goethe, 1808**

Faust is a warning about selling your soul. It was created around the time of the witch trials and Protestant revolution. Accusations around that time were being flung all over the place; everyone was being put on trial for working with the devil. It recounts and teaches the belief that love saves all, however, it also gives caution of working with the devil.

There are many texts on summoning demons, from the ancient thirteenth century to present. There are many black magick grimoires—some were too over the top to really be seriously considered as magical texts; they focused more on the words and theatrics than the down-and-dirty demons. These over-the-top books were written by imaginative people who believed they knew what happened when the witches met the Satan. As an example, note the Le Grand Grimoire. It was translated by A.E. Waite who claimed "this the most fantastic of the texts of the Black Magic cycle, and one of the most atrocious of its class." He does not deny that some of the writings may work (however if you get the English version. be aware it does not contain full text and will work against you), but that they are too dangerous, bordering on criminal, and "the Rites are not reasonable and unsafe."

I am not endorsing any use of the Occult unless you know what you are getting yourself into and are aware of the consequences—I myself do use occult practices to release spirits and free the possessed, but just as I can use the occult for positive, you can unknowingly unleash an entity that could potentially kill you. Be aware that most texts are missing some or all of the incantations and writings that are important to the ritual, which could go against you or cause nothing to happen at all. Unless you know what you are doing, your odds are better playing Russian Roulette.

When most modern Occultists discuss the summoning of demons, they do not necessarily mean the conjuring of physical demonic entities—some consider it the negative parts of your mind, fears you need to face, etc. However, even still, conjuring that part which you fear, or that keeps you depressed, can be just as deadly. I cannot caution you enough, if you decide to engage in Occult activities, you are taking your life and passing it into the hands of an unknown entity, even if it is another aspect of yourself. Not everything can be controlled with words or symbols, especially for those who are just toying with it.

When I go into a home where demonic entities are suspected of haunting, the first thing I look for are any occult books, videos, icons, etc. More often than not I will find one or more of these things lying somewhere around the house and the afflicted will confirm that they had used the item for summoning. Most of the time, they are trying to contact a loved one or friend who has passed, but are unknowing of the danger in opening a portal within the home. Even the most positive of magick when yielded incorrectly can cause disastrous results.

Summoning entities is the most dangerous of practices even if you do know what you are doing. I find that more often than not, these entities they talk about are in fact what would now be considered demonic entities and they act accordingly. As we discussed in an earlier chapter, these inhuman spirits need an invitation, and the spells and chants are just that. You are laying out the black carpet for these creatures.

I have had several people ask me about killing demonic entities through the use of the Occult, and although I myself do use it, I do not suggest anyone trying it without the proper learning and tools. It is as though it is the new trend—you turn on the television and see an occult specialist or exorcist. Most of the occult specialists you see study mainly modern occultism which, as we discussed, does not deal with actual demonic entities, but is about working on and improving the self. And most exorcists do not understand the occult practices that could have created or summoned the demonic entity, therefore, they each miss a large piece of the puzzle and both could be dangerous or fatal to the victim and practitioner.

You do not "kill" demons; demons are energy and it is a scientific and occult fact that energy can neither be created or destroyed, only changed. What in fact you do is cleanse or banish the energy from the home or property. These terms mean very different things; to cleanse is to filter the energy of the demon. It changes it from a negative energy into a positive one through the use of symbols and incantations. To banish the entity is to give it permanent exile from the residence, property, or person. Oftentimes, when dealing with lower demonic entities, it is more useful to cleanse it, where as dealing with larger or higher level entities, it is better to banish because of the time it would take to cleanse—the strength of the demon may be too great to keep it sealed for the process.

** There are many different ways to summon a demon—through words, incantations, symbols and meditation. **

Summoning, cleansing, banishing—all a part of the occult and all dangerous to the ill advised and unlearned. My suggestion is to leave it alone…completely alone. You do not want to end up in a position where you have to call someone (like myself) to help you; it is not a pleasant experience to be demonically haunted. Here is an example from one of my cases:

THE SUMMONING

James was fifteen when he lost his friend Kevin; it destroyed him because they were like brothers and James felt Kevin was the only one who ever understood him. You see, James had a very noticeable speech impediment which caused him to be made fun of often, but Kevin never had, and they had been joined at the hip since the first week of third grade. After Kevin died, James became a loner. He often stayed home, whereas with Kevin, he was always outside, going to the movies or over his friend's house to play videogames.

A few weeks after Kevin passed, James began to dream of his friend. They were laughing, hanging out, and Kevin always mentioned wanting to come back, "We will hang out together again and we'll have fun! I'll protect you from the other guys; I'll be with you all the time," Kevin would say.

Then, one day, James promised to bring him back. "I will find a way, I promise." James was a boy on a mission; he began reading books on necromancy and summoning the dead. Finally, he found a book that talked about an entity you could conjure who would bring someone back to life for you.

James went to his room and shut the door, which was his habit since he had begun to try finding a way to bring Kevin back—he wanted complete privacy. He read through the book and the list of ingredients needed to conjure the entity. Among the necessities was a mirror and chalk. James had some white chalk, and used the mirror on his dresser; the ritual did not need much more, except some herbs and candles, which he was able to get from his allowance from the local craft shop.

At one o'clock in the morning, he began burning the incense, and lit the candles; the book was on his dresser and he stood in front of it looking into the mirror. He began his chant, which was to be said nine times. He stared into the mirror as he invoked the entity—it was supposed to appear in the glass. After the final chant had been said, he continued gazing into the mirror. Slowly, the surface became smoky and opaque; it then cleared. Nothing else happened after that. James went to bed angry that he had failed his friend; that night Kevin didn't come to him.

The next morning, he woke up depressed and forlorn; it was a weekend, so he laid in bed and went over the events of the night before, trying to figure out where he went wrong. A week passed and Kevin still did not come, but Chrissy, James' three-year-old sister was having nightmares every night of what she called *the ugly man*.

James' parents didn't think anything of it, till a month afterward. Little things had been happening around the house, doors opening and shutting on their own, arguments. James sank deeper into depression and began to get to the point where suicide became a possibility for him. His dreams of Kevin began again, but his friend was mean and angry; sometimes he heard Kevin when he was in school, too. It was like his best friend was always putting him down now.

When Christy began the night terrors, the parents took her to a child psychologist. They deemed it just a normal part of childhood and told her parents to comfort her when she needed it, but otherwise, there was nothing they could do. Then one night after a particularly horrible night terror, Christy's mom was sitting in the chair beside her daughter's bed, and she watched in horror as an invisible entity pulled down the comforter and sheets. The mother ran to her husband; when the pair came back in the room, the blankets were back to their original position. The mother knew she wasn't crazy but the father chalked it up to her being over tired. So they both went to sleep and let it be.

I got involved after two months—activity had increased to the point where the family was ready to move out in a moments notice. I decided to sleep over for a night to document the activity. I spent time with the family, discussing the issues they claimed poltergeist activity; the mother talked about a time when she tried to go grab some laundry from her son's room and hearing a dog growling when she reached for the door knob. At one point, she was in the kitchen and she heard something fall to the floor. She went into the living room and her grandmother's Bible had been thrown out of the glass cabinet. Her daughter's night terrors were getting more and more violent with members of the family being killed. Her brother seemed to be one of the main characters in her dreams, usually being the one to commit the acts.

During my time with the family, James was resistant to talk with me, but finally I got the opportunity to talk to him privately. He told me about the loss of his friend, and about the summoning. I asked him to get the book for me and he did. It was a common book, one available at almost any esoteric web site and occult bookstore, and of course as is the case for most of these older writings, there was no Rite written to release the entity.

I recognized the name of the inhuman spirit and knew the way to rid the house of it. I took each family member one by one and cleansed them, releasing them of any connection with the demonic entity. Then I stayed in James' room where the entity's root was and began to the banishing ritual. It took two hours, but the spirit was gone. Afterward, I took James aside and spoke to him about his friend. Later the family opted to have a session with Beckah and Raven, the Ghost Quest mediums, so that James could reconnect with Kevin. Since the time of the banishment, the family has had no more activity, James has been in counseling since to deal with his grief in a more positive way, and he has had no more dreams of his friend, Kevin.

As you can see, even with the best of intention you can bring forth the highest of evils; they will not attack just you, but your family, friends, and acquaintances—anything they can to get to you. When summoning an entity, it is important that you know how to control and release it. If you cannot find these instructions within the book, then **do not** attempt it.

Making a Deal
With a Demon

here are many ways demons try to tempt someone, they are metaphysical beings that proclaim knowledge beyond our comprehension. They are believed to have heightened psychic ability which may allow them to see far into the future, to manifest riches, fame, glory, to find lost treasures, to return a lover, to give all knowledge of the occult, medicine, and war strategy. These are things people would love to have accessible to them. The thing with us as humans is that we are fallible. We make mistakes; sometimes we are impulsive. There have been quite a few accounts in history where people made a pact with the devil or a certain demon and paid for it with their lives. The first recorded pact within the beginning of Christianity was a servant of Senator Proterius of Caesarea. The servant had fallen deeply in love with the senators daughter, but knew there would be no hope due to the position he held within the house. The daughter never noticed him, and this frustrated the servant deeply loved her, so much so in fact that he called upon the Devil and renounced God in order to gain the daughter's hand in marriage. However, according to the history surrounding this particular tale, the servant's soul was saved by the prayer of St. Basil. (Wiemken xxiv).

Here is the prayer in its entirety:

"O God and Lord of the Powers, and Maker of all creation,
Who, because of Thy clemency and incomparable mercy,
didst send Thine Only-Begotten Son and our Lord Jesus Christ
for the salvation of mankind, and with His venerable Cross didst
tear asunder the record of our sins, and thereby didst conquer the
rulers and powers of darkness; receive from us sinful people,
O merciful Master, these prayers of gratitude and supplication,
and deliver us from every destructive and gloomy transgression,
and from all visible and invisible enemies who seek to injure us.
Nail down our flesh with fear of Thee,
and let not our hearts be inclined to words or thoughts of evil,
but pierce our souls with Thy love, that ever contemplating Thee,
being enlightened by Thee, and discerning Thee,
the unapproachable and everlasting Light,

we may unceasingly render confession and gratitude to Thee:
The eternal Father, with Thine Only-Begotten Son,
and with Thine All-Holy, Gracious, and Life-Giving Spirit,
now and ever, and unto ages of ages.

Amen."

There is another big name within the pacts: Pope Honorious III was crowned on August 31, 1216; his predecessor Pope Innocent III had two aims during his papacy—one was to reclaim the Holy Land, the other was to spiritually reform the church. Where Pope Innocent III tried to reach his goal through force and severe punishment, Honorious was kind, compassionate, and lenient. However, he was huge on education. He actually deprived a bishop his office due to illiteracy. He also gave a lot to two universities in Paris and Bologna, both sites of high education at the time, to support theological study so that priests could carry the knowledge to more remote diocese. He also supposedly wrote a grimoire, or magical text, based on the concept that forewarned is forearmed. In this text called the Grimoire of Honorious, he discusses the value of occult knowledge in the Church, and how by summoning or raising demonic entities, one could learn to control them. He uses his faith in God and mixes with it the teachings of King Solomon; it contains invocations of demonic entities for every day of the week. He talked about the priest needing to fast for a certain amount of time and the sacrifice of animals in order to help with the binding of evil spirits.

"Immolated Lamb, be Thou a pillar of strength against demons. Slain Lamb, give power over the Powers of Darkness! Immolated Lamb, grant favour and strength unto the binding of Rebellious Spirits. So be it."

~ Grimoire of Pope Honorious III

The symbology is particularly obvious as Jesus Christ is often referred to as the Lamb of God; this is one of the lesser invocations within the grimoire as it does not summon a demon, but gives the power of binding to the priest. Even though a positive outcome it is still considered occultism.

Now I never endorse summoning any type of entity, but I feel that knowledge cannot do harm, unless you use that knowledge with negative intent, or without researching fully. However, some priests, even Popes in history, took it one step further and fell victim to the temptation of a demon. Now, let's think about this. If someone as pure and godly as a priest or pope could fall victim to these entities, what chance is there for us? A really good one, because as humans we have a tendency to look at past mistakes and draw conclusions on how to protect ourselves from them. Your conclusion should be, "I'm not messing with this stuff!"

Many within the church (and outside) have fallen victim, here are a few well known cases from the past:

Urbain Grandier
(Born 1590 - Died 1634)

Urbain Grandier was a french Catholic priest at the church of Sainte Croix in Loudon. Priests are to take a vow of celibacy, but Grandier didn't take his vows as seriously and involved himself in numerous sexual affairs. Claim was put against him by a convent of Ursuline nuns, who claimed they had been bewitched by him and that he had sent the demon, Asmodai, and others to the convent. To be fair, many modern commentators who have analyzed the life of Urbain Grandier believe that these claims were originally made by the Mother Superior alone, because the priest had rejected the offer to become a spiritual counselor for the convent. Some think that it was because the Mother Superior became obsessed with Grandier, after hearing of some of his sexual exploits. After voicing the fact that he had sent a demon, the other nuns came forward with similar stories, almost in a type of mass hysteria.

Grandier was always living on the edge of right and wrong, and was extremely vocal about his dislike of one particularly powerful church leader named Cardinal Richelieu. Urbain published slanderous letters and verbally attacked him in public. For someone as highly thought of and respected as the Cardinal, he knew that the priest had to be gotten rid of. Somehow, the Cardinal came to find a Devil's Pact signed by Grandier; it is signed by the priest and has been authenticated to have been written by his hand. The Pact was written backwards in abbreviated Latin, signed by Urbain, Lucifer, Leviathon, and others. Nobody can quite prove where the Cardinal got the Pact or if Urbain was forced to do it by the Richelieu, but if you go by the previous claims by the nuns, if we believe them to be truth, it shouldn't come as a surprise that the documents exist. Inevitably, the Cardinal got his wish and rid himself of Father Grandier; the priest was submitted to the extraordinary questioning, a loose term for torturing that over a long time would prove fatal. Grandier never proclaimed guilt, and ended up being burned at the stake on August 18, 1634.

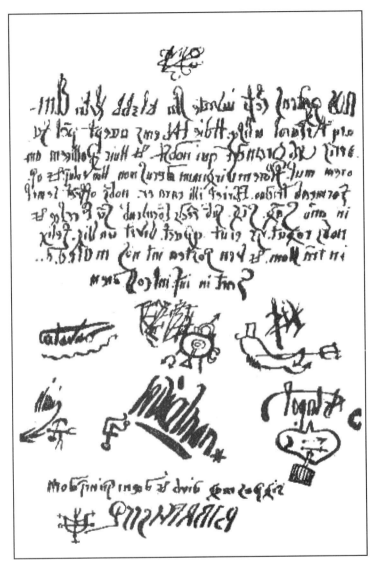

Urbain Grandier's Pact with the Devil.

Transcription of Text (in real form)

mlE ntvL bbzlB ntS entvuj rfcL snetpp soN
tcap tpecca smebah eidh qsila toratsA qta
mecillop ciuh te .e sibon iuq rdnarG brU siredeof
. po te pulov noh nom suced munigriv merolf lum meroma
lemes terffo sboN .re arac illi teirbe oudirt bacinrof
te ealccE as baclucoc sdep bus gis gas ona ni
xilef giv na teviv tcap q ;ture suispi tagor sbon
.D delam son tni aetsop nev te moh art ni
mead ssoc tni fni ni tcaF
sanataS bubezleB rfcL
imilE nahtaiveL htoratsA
mod pcnirp mead te baid gam sop giS
tprcs htrblB

English Translation—Not Abbreviated, Written Forwards:

We, the influential Lucifer, the young Satan, Beelzebub, Leviathan, Elimi, and Astaroth, together with others, have today accepted the covenant pact of Urbain Grandier, who is ours. And him do we promise the love of women, the flower of virgins, the respect of monarchs, honors, lusts and powers. He will go whoring three days long; the carousal will be dear to him. He offers us once in the year a seal of blood, under the feet he will trample the holy things of the church and he will ask us many questions; with this pact he will live twenty years happy on the earth of men, and will later join us to sin against God. Bound in hell, in the council of demons.

Lucifer Beelzebub Satan
Astaroth Leviathan Elimi
The seals placed the Devil, the master, and the demons, princes of the lord.

Baalberith, writer

As I mentioned before, clerics are not immune to the guiles of Satan, in Podlazice Monastery, back in the thirteenth century, there was a story of a Benedictine monk whose crimes against God were so heinous, his brothers were ready to seal him into a wall of the monastery as punishment. But this monk happened to be a wonderful writer of manuscripts and promised to create a book in one night that would bring honor, glory, and esteem to the brothers and their monastery. It would contain all human knowledge up until that point in history, so that night the monk worked furiously, writing, illuminating and illustrating. He could not believe his eyes when he saw the moon reach its peak; he knew he had stretched himself too thin, attempting to write a book which contained so much in so little time and realized that his task would not be completed by the morning. He looked to the Devil to help write his book, and so the demon did appear, giving aid in return for the monk's soul. The entity demanded his mark be made upon the book and so the monk cleverly drew a picture of the Devil into the text.

The manuscript was composed of multiple texts, including the Bible, principles for priests, magical formulas, exorcism rituals, a calendar, medicinal formulary, local and Jewish history, and universal knowledge. Unfortunately, this tale has a sad ending. After being saved from having to die in a wall in the monastery, the monk felt relief, but his mind was never again peaceful. Until he turned to the Holy Virgin looking for salvation, she did agree to help him by absolving him. But just as he was about to receive absolution from his pact, it is said that he died.

The book is kept in a museum in the National Library of Sweden; it is considered the largest written text in the world with over 642 pages, and takes two attendants to move it at 165 pounds. It's named the *Codex Gigas* which literally translates to "Giant Book." It is also known as the *Devil's Bible*, for its depiction of the demon contained within the book. It is an alarming three feet tall, almost twenty inches wide, and nearly nine inches thick. It is a piece of history, occultism, and art; if you could see it in person, I suggest you try. It is a magnificent text.

A OUIJA BOARD'S REALM

or hundreds of years, people have had an avid interest in the afterlife and communication with the deceased. One of the many tools that have been used is the Ouija Board, in German literally meaning "The Yes-Yes Board." Over the past thirty years, through stories, movies, and some personal accounts, the Ouija has gotten a bad reputation for being a harbinger of evil entities. Many people have referred to this wonderful tool as the first wireless communication device—there could be some truth to that. There is such an obsession and craze with Ouijas that the superstitions surrounding them have taken on a life of their own. These beliefs are now called "Ouijastitions."

Let's go back in time to the year 1891. During this time, just around the Victorian era when spiritualism was beginning to take over society, there was a manufacturer called the Kennard Novelty Company who had gotten the inspiration for a Ouija board from a planchette. During the nineteenth century, most individuals used a automatic writing technique called a Planchette to contact spirits from the other side. Each were made out of an oval shaped piece of wood which had a hole in the middle. This wooden piece would rest on rollers and then was placed on a sheet of paper. The user would place a pencil or pen into the hole in the middle of the wood and the spirits would guide the users hand while answering questions. The use of this tool was fun and exciting because you had no control over the writing whatsoever and were channeling the spirit yourself.

Kennard Novelty Company decided to reproduce a more modern method of the planchette, by creating a board with letters, numbers, yes, no, hello, and goodbye. This made the tool much more interactive. William Fuld, an employee of the company, continued making improvements on the board, but unfortunately, the Kennard Company folded. But from them came Will Fuld and his "Best of All" Ouija Board, which was almost a perfect copy of Kennard's board. He then continued on to create new boards, and from there, became the most prominent Ouija Board maker known today. After thirty-five years of success, Mr. Fuld's life came to a tragic end. During a brief drop in sales, some believe he committed suicide by jumping off a three-story building; others say that he was watching a flag pole being replaced and fell three stories to his death. The building was sold on the thirty-ninth anniversary of his death.

In 1966, William Fuld's heirs sold the patent, name, designs, and all to Parker Brothers; Hasbro took over Parker Brothers in the 1990s and have created another new type of Ouija that glows in the dark. They continue to produce them today.

Between the years 1900 to 1960, almost every home had a board. It wasn't until the release of the movie *The Exorcist* in 1972 that Ouija Board superstitions began to take off. It seems even in our day and age, Ouija boards still get a bad reputation. During my lectures or even just sitting around the table talking with friends or family, I have rarely ever heard of a good Ouija board experience—probably because the Ouija sessions gone awry are more entertaining and scary to hear. I mean, isn't that what ghost stories are all about? But for every negative story you have heard, there are probably about forty good stories you haven't. I have experienced both the negative and positive benefits of board work, most of my negative sessions have been the result of playing when I was a teenager, without knowing the rules of the Otherworld and its many portals (the Ouija being a primary example). Here are two stories, both a warning to potential Ouija Board players. In the first is one of my first sessions with the board; the second is a more recent story and, although at some points scary, it does end well. After the stories, we will talk a little bit about how to conduct yourself during a session and some of the other provisions you can take so you make sure one of my terrifying experiences dosen't become one of yours.

A SPIRIT CALLED JAH

As a teenager I always loved hanging out with my friends—this girl, Gina, and I were really close. We decided one afternoon to go and hang out at her boyfriend's apartment for a few hours. Gina was seventeen years old and I'd just turned sixteen; we didn't go there with any kind of intent to use a Ouija board. As we both entered the apartment, a strange feeling quickly made the hair on my arms raise straight up. I blew this feeling off, thinking maybe it was just me being silly. Gina's boyfriend was older than her and lived with a roommate; her boyfriend was home but the guy he shared the apartment with was out at work. Out of the corner of my eye, I saw a bookshelf with some occult writings and I just couldn't resist. At that moment, I was so happy the roommate was out so I could take my time and look over his collection.

No one had noticed what I was doing in the tiny living room; Gina and her boyfriend were in the kitchen getting something to snack on while we hung out. But wouldn't you know, just when I foundd something to take the boredom out of my day, Gina and her boyfriend walked right through the door. I didn't want to get caught, so I quickly made it look like I was leaning on the bookshelf.

"Let's play with the Ouija board," he said.

At this point in my life, I had already had some experience with the occult, but never had any particular interest in the Ouija Board; I had figured it was just a game.

I agreed, thinking anything was better than just sitting around watching the two of them stare at each other.

Now, I wish I hadn't; I figured with all of my studies of the occult I wouldn't scare easy—yeah, right. Big mistake! So I elected to be the "scribe," in other words, I wrote down all the information the board spelled out. I came at it very skeptically; Gina was a little more gullible than me and a lot more nervous. She tentatively placed her fingers upon the planchette alongside her boyfriend's. At first, the board made small circles, then pointed to a bunch of letters that didn't make sense.

"The spirit is getting to know the board," said Gina's boyfriend. I nodded my head like I believed him. After a minute or two of this nonsense, I was ready to do something else. Then Gina said she thought that the planchette was trying to spell something out. Quickly, the piece moved across the board to the J A H. Gina asked for the sex of the spirit, to which it replied it was female. At this point, I gained interest, but still doubted, thinking maybe Gina's boyfriend was pushing the planchette just to have something seem like it happened. So I decided to test this "entity" by asking questions in my head.

Every occultist has some form of "secret name" which is used during ritual; it is a name no one else knows except the occultist and deity. I figured if this spirit were real, it would be able to tell me my secret name. I didn't say anything, just thought it in my head. It answered my question—I just couldn't believe it. I just froze. So I asked a couple more questions in my mind, and again the spirit answered. Gina and her boyfriend were getting a little annoyed with the spirit, not understanding what was going on, because I didn't mentioned I was asking questions.

Suddenly, the planchette started whipping around the board; I couldn't keep up with the writing. Gina and her boyfriend couldn't keep their fingers on the planchette, so we stopped. We just stared at each other in disbelief; Gina was really freaked out and I was just stunned. After a moment or two, we decided to try again, but before the couple's fingers could touch the planchette, it started whipping around and then flew off the board. I was ready to leave at this point, wondering what in the world was in the house. Just as I was thinking about getting up and leaving, there was a loud *BANG* and *CRASH*. We all ran to the kitchen to find out what happened.

When we entered, we saw that all the cabinets were open and the pots and pans were scattered across the floor as if someone was trying to clean out the cabinet. I was ready to bolt, but Gina's boyfriend was one of those macho guys who always had to look tough. He made a noise of disgust and said, "Don't freak, it happens all the time."

After two more minutes of saying goodbye, we walked very quickly out of the building. Things were never right in that apartment, both of the guys living there had issues ever since moving in. One became abusive and controlling, the other deeply depressed and attempted suicide a couple of times. Two months after this incident, Gina broke up with her boyfriend because she couldn't handle the stress of the relationship and the entity.

As a teenager, I never knew about the rules of a Ouija board and just what the consequences might be. Now as an adult, I know the rules and how to protect myself and others from opening the doorway which might invite more then just a spirit in. Many individuals I meet at my lectures love to debate with me about any form of safety using a board. Believe me, protection is the big key, and more often then not, those individuals debating me are the ones who end up calling me to please close the doors they've opened because they played with the Ouija without using protection.

AN OBSESSION GONE WRONG

It was mid afternoon in May when I received a call from a young man who seemed rather worried about his mother. He explained for years his mother had become obsessed with playing the Ouija board. At one point, the woman's son threw all his mother's boards away, but his effort was pointless. Seems this boy's mother had made herself a Ouija board out of paper. Through all these years of playing with the board, the mother had opened doors which allowed many entities other then just spirits to come through. By the time I was called in to investigate, the house was rocking with inhuman and human spirits.

When I sat down with the middle-aged woman, she seemed rather calm and asking, "why was I called?" As I explained why my presence was needed and started my evaluation, asking certain questions—medical, spiritual, and paranormal—I asked if she had any Ouija boards in her home now. She sat quietly for a second almost like a junkie, afraid I would take her drugs away, she nodded and I asked her to please get all boards she still had. There were seventeen paper boards in all and she placed them on the table in front of me. Each paper board was made differently; some letters were made of pencil and other letters were made out of markers. By this time the woman's son had joined us and started to explain some paranormal activity which was going on, like doors slamming shut, phone calls which had static in the back ground and some type of high pitched voice, foul smells, walls that seemed to breath, small black images running quickly past you and many forms of growling.

"How long has this paranormal activity been happening?" I asked.

"Years" he said, "but recently the house has been more active. Sometimes," he said, "my mother will start screaming at me or something I can't see. When my mother is like that, she talks about her new friends which come and go from her paper Ouija boards."

As I took a moment out and walked around the inside of the house, I checked out all the rooms with the escort of the son; he mentioned that his mother has no history of mental illness and is not on any medications. (In my line of work, it is necessary to ask certain medical questions, before ever asking anything that may lead the client to a paranormal or demonic conclusion. If I find it is a medical issue, I refer the individual to a medical professional. Oftentimes, they feel better just knowing it is in their mind and not all around them.) During my walk through, I noticed several hallway mirrors were broken and there were also small round burn marks on the floor.

Before I opened my mouth to question my findings, the son said, "My mother burned some of her small paper Ouija boards here and broke the mirrors." He also stated that his mother thought that by doing this, it would seal up the door which she created. Yes and no. Yes, the doors through these mirrors are now inoperable, but what ever came through them, stayed in the house, and all the other doors were still opened. Even by destroying all the wood and paper Ouija boards would not destroy those entities within the home. They have no connection to the paper boards; their connection is to the operator. Obsession is the first stage of any demonic possession, and it was horribly apparent with my client that she had surpassed that stage and had moved on to infestation, according to the paranormal activity.

If it had just been the mother, I would have questioned her further. However, the son had his own experiences, which led me to believe that the activity was indeed of a supernatural nature.

I proceeded with an exorcism of the home, giving specific instructions that the son be removed from the situation and that the mother understand that after what I did, there would no longer be any activity or phenomena and that the demonic entities would be completely removed. The mother was clearly distraught by the news that these people or beings she trusted so implicitly would not be around for her to communicate with. The procedure took the rest of the day to complete. I started around one in the afternoon; there were a lot of different entity types within the home that had to be dealt with, so it was a slower process than usual. By the time the banishing of these supernatural beings was finished, the client was in tears, finally seeing with a clear mind everything that had happened, how she had been manipulated, and how it had hurt her child. After all of this had occurred, she decided to go to therapy, to reconcile her strained relationship with her son who was still wary about her after the exorcism. They have since reported that no other phenomena has occurred within the home and they are well on their way to regaining their status as a fully functioning, happy family.

HOW TO PROTECT YOURSELF

Ouija Board practitioners will tell you it is important to keep yourself safe above all other things. Like anything else you need to be wary of your emotional state at the time (do not use the Ouija if you are suffering a bout of the blues)—like attracts like. Also, there is a psychic technique of protection called bubbling up, we use it a lot on investigations to protect ourselves from malicious spirits and other entities. It is the practice of envisioning a white pinpoint of light above your head, then it expands and surrounds your body like a cocoon, it is like getting a hug from your favorite relative or friend. Then you envision all of the nasty things in the world that you can and cannot see, coming at you at once and bouncing off this shield and into the universe. This solidifies in your mind the protection is working. The best way to do this when using a Ouija board is to create this barrier through visualization around the home, not just you.

The next step is to be sure that the person you are talking to is a spirit. The thing that you must remember as a practitioner of the board is that demonic entities know everything about you except what you are thinking in that moment. So you ask a simple question such as, "What number am I thinking of?" if the answer is correct then you have a spirit, incorrect, well it may be something else entirely. If you find that the entity does not give you a satisfactory answer then stop using the board immediately.

Demonic entities have been known to show themselves as relatives or friends who have passed, but so do other spirits, so this question technique is very important. If they give you the correct answer, don't trust just yet that is your mother or an old family friend. Get specific with the questions you ask, things only you would know. Spirits can pick up on your thoughts, but more likely, the planchette will start to move erratically around the board giving various letters or "jabber" with no meaning behind it. When this occurs, stop the session. The protection should keep negative spirits at bay, but never take chances with the board. The negative spirits can sometimes be just as bad as demonic ones.

PART III
EXORCISM

FACING DOWN THE DEVIL

his may be the hardest part of my job; everything depends upon my next move. An individual's life and soul are resting in the palm of my hands. In most exorcisms I am dealing with an individual who is either possessed with a form of demonic entity or either thinks that they are possessed. Once I begin an exorcism, it can NOT be stopped. The demonic entity must never have a chance to gain that upper hand on the exorcist. No matter how much one prepares or studies for an exorcism, it will always feel like it's never enough.

I know most of us were brought up to believe that only clergy can or could do exorcisms. But now we are in the twenty-first century and a lot has changed since the old days. I do not follow the churches way or report to any priest or bishop. This tends to raise eyebrows among some people, but my success rate using my method is 100 percent effective and is much safer and faster.

Exorcisms are not like what you see in the movies. I have in the past assisted in a couple of them with a dear friend of our family who was a Roman Catholic priest. He was present to conduct the Rites for the person; one of the main reasons I was there was to observe and learn. The exorcism was a long process, and you could see the battle of wills between the demon and the exorcist. It enthralled me; that was one of my many "*aha*" moments—when I knew this was what I wanted to do with my life. I wanted to help these people the best way I knew how.

I have no real issues with the church, if they can help someone, then more power to them. But watching this person suffer in agony for hours killed me. You will never hear me claim that I am an exorcist for God, or that I am in any way an ordained minister of any Christian religion. I am an occultist.

So how does occultism signify with exorcism? Many believe that only the words of Jesus Christ or their particular Deity work, and that is simply not true. There are religions older the Christ, belief systems older than Christ. What happens when an exorcist runs across a demonic entity or evil spirit that is not from the Christian religion; would the words of Christ work? What if a Buddhist monk tried to exorcise a Catholic demon; would that work? Maybe, but it's not guaranteed. I have seen cases where the demonic entity was not affected by the words of the clergy's faith. Who hasn't heard of exorcisms that resulted in someone's death? As an occultist, you work with a mainly neutral system and this allows one to alter the symbolisms that are necessary to that religion's demon or evil spirit.

The main thing to know with exorcism is not only your faith and beliefs, but that of the client. Even though one may be possessed, the demon never controls the soul and so the victims energy and want of freedom coincides with the exorcists want to release. Using symbols of that religion—the one the demonic entity recognizes as more forceful than itself—creates the necessary "push" to release the entity from the person, place, or object. I am not the first to use this method; it has been used again and again. It is even being used as we speak, by others. I believe in the faith of all the religions, for we all share the same Deity in essence—it is the Divine love, peace, and positive energy inherent in all, and in nature. Again I am not endorsing that you try it, or that you attempt it without proper training; that would be like trying to attempt a Catholic exorcism without having gone to seminary. If you don't know what you are doing, do not do it!

This is a difficult field, one that can scar you mentally and physically. It is not always easy to banish the entity, even with the knowledge behind you. You can never be prepared enough. Why would any exorcism last more then a day? That is torture for anyone who claims to be, or really is, possessed. There has been far to many deaths related to these types of exorcisms and something needs to be done about it. My method, using occult magical seals, draws the demonic entity out of an object or person and is painless. The magical seals which I use are not evil, but contain sacred symbols and writings, that many different entities recognize as powerful. It slips our minds that demons are older then man and can possess anything it pleases. It is in fact rare to see a true demonic infestation; I get called on many cases that turn out to be everything BUT demonic. There are many other things to consider such as, mental illness, spirits, mixing medications, etc. Demonic possession is even rarer; if you ever hear an exorcist say they have done an outrageous number of exorcisms, then they are either being untruthful or performing the rituals with no actual need for them. They could in fact be dealing with a spirit, a schizophrenic (which would cause the person to possibly develop another personality altogether), or someone who is psychically gifted and doesn't know it.

Exorcists and demonologists both tread on thin ice when dealing with a possible demonic haunting; there are certain things an exorcist will do to confirm the presence of a demonic entity. If the reaction that is expected does not take place, then it is not demonic, but could be a possible spirit attachment. The evaluation and steps of pre-exorcism are so important—you need to be 100 percent sure.

When I was growing up, my family was very active in our local church. My mother used to have the local priest, Father B., over all the time to visit; he had a lot of influence over my life when I was young—I looked up to him. Before I was a year old, Father B. had a brush with a group of Satanists. They actually practiced their rituals deep in the woods behind a Catholic school; the priest ended up booting them out after many attempts of telling them to leave and getting a "yeah, right" response. After the group finally moved on for good, Father B. blessed the area to rid it of any evil the Satanists might have conjured. Looking back, I am not sure if they were actually Satanists, pagans, or something else entirely, but Father B. and the nuns were convinced they were evil.

We were all very involved in the Roman Catholic Church while I was growing up; my parents were on the committee (they were so proud to be in a respected position within the Church; they felt they were doing good work and I believe they were) and my brother was altar boy for many years. I remember going to church and being fascinated with the sermons and watching the priests go through the rituals at the altar every Sunday. I remember there were times when the Gregorian monks would come and conduct a ceremony—I used to go home and feel just charged with energy and the feeling that I could do anything, it was so powerful.

My fascination with both the occult and rituals of the Roman Catholic Church compounded my calling and determination to develop a way to do exorcisms safely and efficiently. Throughout time, many cultures have had different people who have conducted exorcisms, from priests, to sorcerers. To understand the meaning and power behind these rituals we must turn back the dial of time and look to the earliest known exorcists.

HISTORY OF EXORCISM

umerians seem to have the oldest reference to demonic possession, the local "Ashipu" (sorcerers) would perform the rites and rituals needed to banish the evil entities lingering inside of the body and mind of the possessed.

Josephus, an ancient Jewish historian, claimed that God enabled King Solomon to exorcise and control the demons. "God enabled Solomon to learn that skill which expels demons, which is a science useful and sanative to men. He composed such incantations also, by which distempers are alleviated, and he left behind him the manner of using exorcisms, by which they drive away demons so that they never return." Josephus also spoke of Solomon's tradition of exorcism through the use of seals and incantations which were still utilized by such people as Eleazar, who helped to rid demons from Vespasian, his sons, captains, and army. It is believed he used a ring that has a root in it to pull the demonic entity from the nose of the afflicted. When the entity was captured, he would walk over to a bowl of water and seal the entity inside. He would then overturn the bowl, so the entity would be soaked back into the earth.

In the *Codex Pseudepigraphus of Fabricus*, there are still some supposed fragments of Solomon's incantations and the mention of mandrake root which is believed to be the root used in the exorcism—although this has not been confirmed so please do not try to fend off a demon with a mandrake root. There was also an exorcist named Tobit, the father of Tobias, a Jewish hero; it was believed by the seventeenth century Dutch scholar Grotius that Hebrews believed all diseases that could have been natural were in fact of demonic influence. You can look up many of these facts in Balthasar Bekkers book which has been almost forgotten, called Le Monde Enchanté (1694). It consists of four volumes and discusses the importance and necessity of exorcism.

Mr. Bekker also discussed an instance where Jews tried to ward off the evil influence of Lilith, whom some within the Jewish community believed to be the wife of Lucifer. In the book *Thisbi*, Elias discusses the 130 years prior to Eve's arrival and marriage to Adam, saying that Adam was visited by female devils whose names were Lilis (Lilith), Ogére, Machalas, and Naome. Adam was weak and mated with the she-devils; the demons gave birth to evil spirits. In Judaism, they go by the Kabbalah and it speaks of a group of spirits called "Dybbuk." These seem to be the only ones with the ability to possess or control the human spirit. The term demonic entity does not factor into the equation of their religious beliefs.

Hinduism is similar to the Judaic belief of spirits not demons; they use the Athrava Veda, one of the Veda's or Holy Books which contains secrets related to both magic and medicine. Let's speak now about the most recognized religion with demonic influences, Catholicism and Christianity. By Canon Law, only an ordained priest is able to conduct an exorcism, and only with the local Bishop's permission. Since we are talking about the Church, why not discuss the greatest Occultist and Exorcist in their history? Jesus.

In Matthew 8:28-34, it says, *"Jesus sent a herd of demons from two men into a herd of two thousand pigs."* How does he do this? Is it a miracle or magic.

In Matthew 9:32-34, it says, *"Jesus made a demon-possessed, mute man speak, the Pharisees said it was by the power of Beezlebub."*

I believe Jesus was one of the greatest Occultists to ever live. He turned water to wine, controlled weather, raised the dead, and exorcised demonic entities through the use of words, gestures, and symbols. These are occult practices used in every mainstream religion. Jesus also healed the sick. Again, this all was done through spoken words (incantations) and laying of the hands. Jesus made way for the Christian faith, and in the Middle Ages, their belief in the demonic realm came to peak. There were more documented Rituals of Exorcism than in any other period of Christian religious history.

Exorcists within the Catholic Church only made up one small part of the Order. When they were ordained, the priest would basically read them their duties and then imbue them with the power of laying hands and words to exorcise the energumens (demons). In the 1600s, there was a handbook written; it was the most complete book of Exorcism Ritual and Practice consisting of 1,300 pages entitled *Thesaurus Exorcismorum et Conjurationum*. It covered every aspect of the exorcism, including pre-exorcism where not only the demon but the body underwent a series of torture. It was done in the hope of making the demon so uncomfortable that it would leave on its own.

There were eight exorcisms to the method discussed in the *Exorcismorum et Conjurationum*—the pre-exorcism was followed by prayers, adjurations, psalms, and lessons; then followed the post-exorcisms, eight in all. The first few were used to determine if the demon still had possession of the soul and body. If that was the case, then the priests would create a doll or effigy of what they believed the demon to look like and inscribe its name upon the bottom of it. They would then bless a fire by making the sign of the cross and using holy water, then throw the effigy into the fire. After this came two other exorcisms of which were asking for God's prayer and prayers of thanks. They also discussed the exorcism of seductive spirits like incubi and succubi, releasing demons from possessed homes and driving away demonic storms which consisted of throwing various herbs into a fire to scare the inhuman spirit away. Sounds like occultism to me!

The use of effigies, such as wax dolls, cloth, clay, or corn husk dolls are particular to many of the old religions—witchcraft (they refer to them as Poppets) and Santeria or Voodoo all use these methods to obtain wishes or to rid oneself of a spirit or person.

There are herbs that are specific to the use of exorcism; this is not an original Christian thought. Again, it hails back to older times. Mullien is used in many instances as a herb of exorcism. So is frankincense and myrrh; these two ingredients are actually considered resins, not herbs, however they are often used in cleansing and to sanctify a certain area where magic or ritual is to take place. Dragon's Blood is a resin from a tree that is often used for protection. The throwing of herbs into a fire is again not a Christian original; fire is considered an element of transformation and cleansing. This is a very old belief that you will still find with many of the practitioners of neo-paganism and other old religions.

Possessed women were to be handled in a special way by the priests of the old Roman Catholic Church, because they felt that the demon would use the woman's charms against the cleric performing the exorcism. They also had to be aware of the art of deception that the demons had mastered. If the demon refused to reveal its name, it would be fumigated by holy incense like a roach until it conceded according to the "Flagellum Daemonum".

If the inhuman entity persisted in remaining within the body, the priests were instructed to verbally antagonize the demon. After the harsh words were spoken, and if the entity still refused to reveal it's name (which was needed before beginning any exorcism), they would antagonize the inhuman spirit further by calling it the worst names they knew and treating it to another round of fumes.

The Catholic Church had an exorcism for everything. They believed, much like the Jewish community we discussed earlier, that almost everything was linked to a demonic influence including retardation or slowness of the mind, and they created a potentially effective remedy for the exorcism of this ailment. They believed that by mixing a small bottle of holy water with three drops of holy wax and having it drunk by the afflicted on an empty stomach, this would in fact cure the victim of the inhuman entity causing the disease.

During this era, it was believed that any unusual behavior, either by man, woman, child, or animal, could constitute possession. However, more than not, these exorcisms ended in death, either by the ritual itself or to free the soul of the possessed. The Church believed that by killing the person before the demon could completely take over, released the soul back to God and they would still be free to go to Heaven. Animals were also tortured by Rites of Exorcism. The cat species was almost wiped out by their fervent belief of purifying by fire. They would throw the animals into the flames in the belief that it "cleansed" the animal of the demonic entity. These animals were not the only fatalities—and it still happens today.

DEATH AND EXORCISM

ue to different types of exorcisms throughout history and all over the world by various religions, many have died. Most people in our modern age of science and reason, with the Church rarely conducting exorcisms and with recognition of mental illness and disease, have come to believe that these religious rituals are a thing of the past. However, I beg to differ. Listed below are several cases which are now made public, showing the death and danger of these rites. Some of the exorcism victims I present to you are in fact as recent as 2007. Most of these cases were done through various churches or by family members.

DEATHS RELATED TO EXORCISMS:

Here is list of just some of those souls who died by starvation, being beaten to death, suffocation, torture, and crucifixion.

Age: 24 year old male
Died: 1976
Country: Germany
Cause: Pneumonia, Starvation
Exorcist: A Father and Pastor of a Church

Age: 25
Died: 1995
Country: United States
Cause: Beaten to Death by 2 Attackers Struck 50 times each
Exorcist: A leader of the Jesus-Amen Ministries

Age: Unknown
Died: 1995
Country: United States
Cause: Beaten to death during an all night exorcism by husband and parishioners of a Methodist Church
Exorcist: Husband (a reverend)

Age: 17
Died: 1998
Country: United States
Cause: Suffocated with a plastic bag
Exorcist: Mother and Sister (began practices of Santeria shortly before incident)

Age: 17
Died: 2000
Country: New Zealand
Cause: Exorcist sat on chest and bounced on her body; after six hours, he strangled her in the hope that once dead, the demons would leave her and she could be resurrected
Exorcist: A Pastor of a cult

Age: 8
Died: 2004
Country: United States
Cause: Suffocation due to Hemphill laying on the body. Child was autistic and they believed they could "heal" the illness through the exorcism.
Exorcist: A school maintenance worker who spent the rest of his time preaching at his brother's storefront church.

Age: 23
Died: 2005
Country: Romania
Cause: Bound to a cross, gagged with a towel and left for three days without food or water. She died of suffocation and dehydration.
Exorcist: A monk who was reported as saying: "God has performed a miracle for her, finally Irina is delivered from evil."

Age: 20
Died: 1992
Country: United Kingdom
Cause: Starved of food and sleep for eight days. Made to eat chili powder, had seventeen broken bones and three cuts between her breasts.
Exorcist: Two Muslim Holymen

Age: 22
Died: 2007
Country: New Zealand
Cause: Drowned in a large amount of water held in plastic containers
Exorcist: Family trying to free her from a Maori curse or makutu

Age: 2
Died: 1995
Country: Canada
Cause: Her parents and grandmother thought she was possessed by a demon, so they attempted an exorcism. They forced her to drink huge quantities of water. They were charged with a crime.
Exorcist: Mother and Neighbor

Age: 5
Died: 1997
Country: USA
Cause: Tied down and forced to swallow toxic potion with mouth taped shut; because of her tantrums her exorcists believed her possessed.
Exorcist: Mother and Grandmother

Age: 38
Country: Thailand
Died: 1996
Cause: Beaten with a dried stingray tail by her shaman, because the family saw it as a way to rid evil spirits. She fled the shaman but he abducted her and continued till she died.
Exorcist: The Family Shaman

Age: 5
Died: 1996
Country: United States
Cause: Whipped with a cheeseboard for two hours.
Exorcist: Mother and two friends all high on methamphetamines

These are only a few of the thousands of exorcism victims; you can learn more about these fatalities by checking out the websites in the resource appendix. It is totally unacceptable that so many who were already in pain had to suffer. Most of the deaths could have been prevented with the proper care and understanding of someone who has dealt with those afflicted either by demonic possession or mental illness. Most of the exorcists, whether by priest or not, have led to people being jailed for their practices. However, that has not stopped other radical groups from maintaining the old practices of beating and torturing a possession victim to make the demonic entity uncomfortable enough to leave on its own. But as you can also see from this list, most of the people performing the exorcism have some sort of mental illness themselves, either causing a congregation to suffer mass hysteria in the belief that one of their own is tainted by the devil, or by the use of illegal drugs. Every time I hear of a death by exorcism, I can do nothing but honor the lost and wish I had been there to help them. Awareness needs to be raised about the ratio of exorcism deaths. Exorcisms can be done safely to the benefit of the victim. Death in this way is torture and needless.

DEMONIC POSSESSION
VS. PSYCHOLOGY

 ossession: It's when a foreign spirit that is not original to the body enters it against the will of the soul. Whether it is spirit or demonic does not matter; it is still possession. There is a fine line between possession and psychosis. Finding the balance between the two is an art in itself. There are many medications that can cause hallucinations, not to mention the illegal drugs, and it is important to know which is which. There are over 145 known causes for hallucinations, including diseases, sleep deprivation, epilepsy, schizophrenia, cocaine, and other substance abuse, cataracts, Bell mania, and Bipolar disorder, just to name a few.

There are cases which I personally have investigated which involved individuals with some form of a mental disorder. One case had both negative spirits and demonic entities taking residence within that individual's home. And there are those cases where it is plainly relevant that the individual is mentally unstable, and only professional medical help is needed.

Your environment, emotions, and body are very important and can in fact trigger hallucinations, especially when under extreme fatigue and stress. It causes misfire within the mechanism of the brain that distinguishes conscious perception and memory-based perception. The hallucinations can appear through visions, voices and sounds, haptic hallucinations (also known as tactile feeling), tastes, and smells. You can also experience hallucinations when you begin to fall asleep, British Journal of Psychiatry found that thirty-seven percent of the 4,972 people they surveyed experienced this phenomena, and twelve percent experienced it upon waking.

Sleep deprivation or physical exhaustion can actually blur the lines between wakefulness and sleep, thus you enter a middle time where the two may combine causing intense hallucinations. My job as a demonologist is to discover the cause of these hallucinations or experienced phenomena through research and discussion with the client. I have an evaluation form that I go through—demonic hauntings are so rare, maybe one in one thousand are true demonic hauntings, and because of this, I keep my questions open ended. If they are truly haunted by inhuman spirits, they will let me know through their personal experiences.

One of the top questions I have on my evaluation form is: Do you suffer from mental illness? If not I still ask my next question: What medications do you take? Over the counter medicines like antihistamines, and even Advil, have been known to cause hallucinations. I believe it is important for every paranormal group, not just the demonologist to have access to a list of drugs, both illegal, over the counter, and prescribed that could cause these various types of hallucinations. Here are some other medications I have gathered at the website wrongdiagnosis.com that have hallucinatory side-effects if taken in large doses or not following doctors recommended prescription:

- Amobarbital and Secobarbital
- Amoxapine
- Broncaid Dual Action
- Bactrim
- Carbex
- Catapres Tablets
- Demolox
- Dopram Injection
- Enoxacin
- Etrafon
- Flumadine
- Fuxen
- Naprodil
- Pseudovent
- Vivactil
- Vicks Dayquil Allergy Relief 4 Hour Tablet
- Zantac 75

These are just some of the 800 known medications to cause hallucinations. But this varied group of medications is not the only cause of perceived paranormal activity. There is in fact a book of psychology codes and mental illnesses; inside you will read codes for all sorts of mental disabilities and diseases—there is even an illness called demon mania, where a person believes they are possessed by multiple demons. Unfortunately, there is no proof that this is truly a mental issue or a paranormal one.

Not every illness is so hard to distinguish from a haunting though.

Sometimes, it is obvious when people are mentally ill versus haunted, but even after nineteen years within the field, I can be fooled. So it is important to be 100 percent sure, because if you decide that someone is possessed and in fact it is a mental illness say, DID (disassociate identity disorder) or schizophrenia, you could be feeding into the illness, strengthening it, which could set back the ill person's progress with their psychiatrist or therapist. Back in the Medieval ages, they believed that everything was caused by demonic activity, and even till today, there are still people out there who assert that autism, mental illness, and other diseases are caused by evil spirits or demonic entities. Here is a list of some of the obvious signs of paranoia, schizophrenia and other mental illnesses:

Schizophrenia-Delusions

These are false beliefs even though there is strong evidence that the beliefs held are false. It's like saying the sky is blue, and someone else says, "No, it's purple." But it really is blue. Still, you cannot get that other person to realize the fact, even though there are thirty other people agreeing with your belief of the sky's color. But delusion is in fact a broad term covering many different types of this affliction explained in the listings below.

Paranoid Delusions

Persecution; "everyone is out to get me," "the FBI has bugged my house." Even though you pull apart the home looking for these bugs and there are none, they will continue to trust in their beliefs and may come to the fact that you are with *them*.

Delusions of Reference

Things around the person are believed by him/her to be directly related. Things around the person such as televisions, photos, radios are talking to the person or about them— sometimes with personal messages.

Delusions of the Body

The person believes that there is something wrong with their body, either a terrible illness or something has been implanted within them, such as alien tracking devices.

Delusions of Grandeur

Belief that the person has special powers, is famous— royalty etc.

Hallucinations

May include some or all of the five senses.

Muddled or Incompetent Speech

Rambling speeches and monologues, often including the person talking to themselves or someone around them. Horribly disorganized, they switch from subject to subject erratically, typically not making much sense.

Trance like or Disorganized Behavior

Person will seem as though in a stupor, or manic fashion. They can also become rigid as a board or extremely flexible physically.

Disassociative Identity Disorder

Previously called Multiple Personality Disorder, DID is a chronic and potentially fatal mental illness, although with the right psychologist and medication, many go on to live healthy and productive lives. Many people who have D.I.D present symptoms of an array of different mental illnesses/ A person may show signs of depression, but it may in fact be that one of his/her other personalities is relieving past issues and feeling the emotions of it.

Self-Injury

Many people who suffer from this disorder are prone to self-mutilation and attempting suicide.

Mood Swings

Their moods are erratic and can go from being incredibly happy to incredibly depressed in a short amount of time.

Compulsions: A person with this disorder may create rituals or compulsions as a way to deal with stress. Typically, when they are agitated, they have triggers specific to heir rituals or compulsion such as a word or behavior, which will cause them to begin their compulsion. An example of a compulsion is to check the doorknob ten times before leaving the home.

Flashbacks or intrusive memories

A high percentage of DID patients admit to being abused as children and the fragmentation may be a result of this; they create alternate personalities to deal with the trauma. But even still, sometimes, these memories will make themselves apparent to the person.

AUDITORY AND VISUAL HALLUCINATIONS

Trances and O.B.E.

OBE is an out-of- body experience; many DID patients refer to feeling as though the are watching a movie of their life. They are also subject to trance-like states, and the feeling of being "pulled" out of their body is not uncommon as another personality takes over.

Sleep disorders

Such as insomnia, night terrors, and sleepwalking.

Amnesia

As different personalities take over, the original person may have moments of blackouts. Most of us cannot recall the first three to five years of life, however those with DID commonly cannot remember the time between ages six and eleven.

Mania

A severe condition characterized by extremely elevated mood, energy, disorganized, or unusual thought patterns and sometimes a type of psychosis.

Excessive Behavior

Abuse of drugs and alcohol, spending sprees, excessive exercise, excessive, and over exaggerated laughter.

Excess of Energy

Rapid movement and speech, hyperactivity, talking a lot, reduced need for sleep.

Mood Swings

Anger, aggression, euphoria—the change can occur rapidly and without notice.

Distractedness

The person may display obvious symptoms of ADHD, such as the distractedness, inability to focus, and hyperactivity.

Delusions

Typically, the delusions are of grandeur like we spoke of in schizophrenia; the person believes they have special powers or are famous.

chart is NOT meant to be used in diagnosis of any mental
.r but to give an example of how complicated it can be to in fact
ɔwn a demonic attack or a mental illness**

These are the three most common types of mental illness cases that
.n called into work with. As you can see, with some of these symptoms,
.hey are obvious of mental illness. But some of these conditions contain
characteristics of demonic influence; usually if someone has seen a
psychologist, they are open about it—some will even allow you to
speak with their psychologist or therapist by signing a confidentiality
release form which will allow you to get a deeper understanding of
any possible conditions, either medical or paranormal, that the client
is dealing with.

It is important for any demonologist to recognize the benefits of
having a psychologist on retainer, so that if you suspect mental illness
and the victim has not yet sought out help, you may point them in the
right direction, or get a psychological analysis of the client's mental
state so you know how to proceed with the victim. It is important to
always look for the mundane before assuming the supernatural.

Even still as I write this, science has not been able to link all of
the characteristics and phenomena of possession with one disease, or
even a couple. Maybe at some point down the road, they will find a
biological reason for why the possessed act as they do. But until it can
be proven that it is natural, I must continue my work. Part of the human
condition is to rationalize what we can't understand, much like a father
explaining away a monster in his son's closet. But still science and its
slew of professionals have not been able to put a disease or biological
reason on the most obvious of symptoms of demonic possession,
such as levitation, wounds that appear on the victim out of no where
(documented with proof of it not being self-inflicted or from any other
source), knowledge of other languages that were not previously known
or spoken by the individual, and expanded psychic abilities.

Also, science has not yet been able to prove the reason as to why
the room where individual resides may be at a considerably lower
temperature than the rest of the home (even when the heat is on), writing
and sounds that occur within the room without any physical source, and
the moving of objects, again with no physical force to be seen.

Earlier we discussed how many religions believed that all illnesses
were a result of evil spirits or inhuman entities, so now we must take
a second out and thank the medical community for making it easier
(sometimes) to distinguish between mental illness and some effects of
demonic activity. But, until they can explain away all of these other
phenomena which occur around the victim, they have still not as of
yet made a concrete case against it in my mind.

PART IV
FIELD GUIDE

STAGES OF DEMONIC ATTACK

INVITATION

his is the first stage of "welcome" without the proper knowledge; you just pulled out the red carpet and invited demonic entities into your home. How did this happen? So many people don't understand that some board games are more then just a board game. Take the Ouija board, as mentioned earlier; originally, this game was designed just for the fun of pretending to contact spirits. We all have played with one, but how many people, before playing, protect themselves, or the area they are in? Thought so. By not protecting oneself, the door to a negative spirit or worse demonic world has just opened.

Let's now talk about different forms of occult and magical books. There are a ton of great occult and magical books that have been written. Some more then others have great power when the words on the pages are said out loud. A lot of antique occult and magical books are very powerful, yet sometimes a line or an important word is left out. Not because the author wants to be sneaky and keep all the secrets to themselves, but because those words are *that powerful*. Let me just say, there are those occult and magical books out there which still have all magical words printed or written in the book, but even with those, you must be cautious.

Oftentimes, these books will tell you that (for example) "this chant is for love." You don't think about it; it's something you want. What is the harm? So you buy the magical book and start speaking or chanting those magical words out loud, without the knowledge of what could happen. Two days later, the guy or girl you want is on your doorstep, begging for you to take them back, or take them out for the first time. It worked! Usually, these texts are in a different language, even if the instructions are in English. It's kind of like signing a legal document—would you sign it before you read it? If you aren't thinking clearly, maybe, but when you just sign or do something without thinking, what usually happens? It comes back to bite you on the butt.

Casting spells and chanting is awesome if you know what you are doing, and it can lead to really good things and be beneficial to everyone, if you know what you are doing.

I also want to discuss a great subject called "Summoning." Summoning books are wonderful if read and used in a correct manner. Yet, time and time again, I get calls from people who misused a "summoning" book and now have demonic activity in their home. A lot of older "summoning" books do not give instructions on safety. NEVER speak words out loud to summon any demonic entity, unless you are experienced. I am not kidding! When an individual who is inexperienced speaks words of summon, you not only just opened that demonic door, but you called upon that particular demon to enter your home. That demonic entity will only wait a second before figuring out that you don't know anything about what you are doing and they are just happy to take possession of, rip apart your family, take away your friends, and leave you a broken shell of yourself.

Life is going an opposite way for you and witchcraft seems to be a great way to change it to your liking. Witchcraft is not a game that you can just use to fit your life or fix ones' problems. I encourage reading and learning on the subject of witchcraft, but like I have mentioned before, learn about safety first and how to protect oneself. Within witchcraft, there are helper spirits—if you pick up a book at your local store about magic, there will be something about these entities written in the pages. I have gotten multiple phone calls from victims of demonic hauntings, who told me they had used these spells, and the spirit they summoned did indeed want to help...for a price. I have come across individuals who had changed the magical words to their liking and nothing happened. Until, the demonic activity started. If interested in witchcraft, there are many great schools and classes available on the Internet, and there are new resources popping up everyday. Just open your eyes, they are there and those who are already involved in the Craft can and will help you. Just remember, protect yourself or you'll be having unwanted guests staying over your house and soon I'll be getting a call to help.

There are times when forms of negative energy can play a role in "welcoming" demonic entities into one's home or life. Demonic entities thrive on individuals who are in depression, abusive relationships, severe drug users, mentally or physically ill, and living in a negative environment. When there is a spark of negativity, whether in the home, body, or mind, it is like a foghorn to the demonic entities—drawing them from the depths of evil for a chance to steal your soul. Those who are close to dying or committing suicide are the easiest prey. This is the demonic entity's last-ditch effort to steal the individual's soul.

INFESTATION

So, you aren't quite sure yet, but something happened! All of a sudden, strange occurrences start occurring around the home and no one has a clue as to what's going on. The demonic entities are moving in, and soon, your home will be their home. It starts slowly at first, and most individuals might think it's their mind playing tricks on them. This is a normal response. Here is a list of the most common demonic activity to look out for:

COMMON DEMONIC ACTIVITY SIGNS

- Foul smells
- Religious objects disappear or desecrated
- Teleporting large objects
- Stacking (furniture such as chairs, tables)
- Knocks
- Growling
- Spontaneous fires
- Levitation
- Sensation of wind while being indoors
- Scratching sounds
- Black cloud-like forms
- Dark shadows
- Being woken up at three a.m.
- Apparitions
- Heavy breathing

Now think about these entities as a completely separate race—they breed. Yes really, they do. They are like roaches in a slum apartment: Once you see one, there are fifty more behind it. Right now, it's just the little things; they aren't ready to take you on completely yet. They just want to get to you a little bit. They will do unnatural things in an almost natural way. You will come home and there will be a fire in the house—oh no, did you leave the stove on? Nothing horrible, yet. Right now they are testing their limits, seeing how hard they have to push to get under your skin.

OPPRESSION

Now it's time to party—they are in your house, even your room; they are the monster under your bed waiting for you to crawl in at night. They are affecting not just you, but your family. Everyone is now in the line of fire. Put your hard hats on because this is war. Family members begin to argue on a regular basis, tension starts to build within the home. Now it's all about separation; they are going to drive you crazy, literally. Divide and conquer; yes, it is fun scaring your family, but their main objective is ultimately *you*. You invited them here, and now you will entertain them. They traveled a long way; now you have to pay for it.

You will see things, hear things, feel things that are out of the norm. You may one day come home from work to see your wife sleeping with another man; you may freak out and shoot them both, only to realize you have been standing in the kitchen the whole time, and your wife was cooking dinner. It never happened, but you though it did. It makes you suspicious, so you start questioning your wife, getting a little paranoid. Eventually, your wife decides she is taking the kids to stay with her mother for a little bit. Now you are alone. Now the fun really starts.

Demonic entities will work on you all at once, mentally, physically, and spiritually. They want you hopeless and helpless. They may boost your psychic abilities, but it is always to their benefit. They will show you things and tell you things that you never wanted to know. They will cut you, burn you, torment you, but you may never be fast enough to get the proof that it happened. You may get the chills, but it's more than the chills. It could be ninety-five degrees in the middle of a summer heat wave and you are feeling sweat pants and a jacket kind of cold. It never goes away. They want you to feel like there is no help, no way, that there is nothing you can do but submit.

The demonic entities are trying to break the individuals "will" down; they can never own your soul, but they will do what they have to, to make sure they keep up their quota—even if that means making you commit the ultimate sin.

At this point, things are beyond denial; something is definitely going on. But can you admit it? Would you tell someone else? It may be that most of your friends already think you are crazy and your family is torn apart. This is typically when I get called in, usually with a sentence starting, "Listen, please, I'm really not crazy..."

Other people just move, but what they don't realize is that demons will move with them.

POSSESSION

This is it, the final point, the deciding moment. Will you totally submit, or keep on trying to fight? This is the last stage of demonic attack. They have beaten your will to a pulp (or so they think), you have become possessed and are no longer in control of your body and mind. Your soul has shrunken back into your body and has let another driver take the wheel. What are you going to do? The only solution now is having an exorcism done—in order to save the person's soul and restore the victim's body back as it once was, there must be an exorcism. Here are some signs of possession:

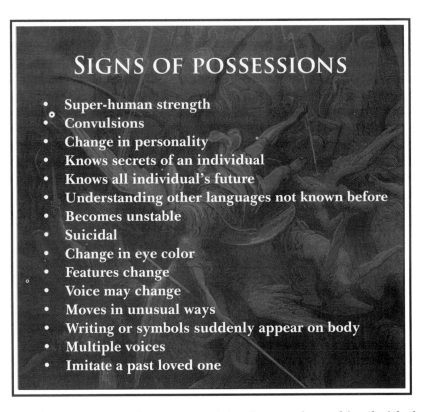

SIGNS OF POSSESSIONS

- Super-human strength
- Convulsions
- Change in personality
- Knows secrets of an individual
- Knows all individual's future
- Understanding other languages not known before
- Becomes unstable
- Suicidal
- Change in eye color
- Features change
- Voice may change
- Moves in unusual ways
- Writing or symbols suddenly appear on body
- Multiple voices
- Imitate a past loved one

With luck, love, and your own spiritual strength combined with the faith of the exorcist, your family, and friends together, you will cast out the evil entity. It is important here that I stress that although the person may be possessed, the demon does not under any circumstance control the soul. The biggest part of the exorcism is reaching the human soul, and helping it to realize it has the power to rid itself of the demon. It still has will, and if wanted badly enough, with enough faith, it along with the exorcist, can expel the demon from the body.

EVALUATING THE CAUSE

s you read before in Part 2: Exorcism, psychology takes a big role in demonic possession and therefore, you must have a resource you can use that will be quick and easy for the client. I use evaluation forms for my clients and often I have a psychologist on hand to consult with. This is a priceless resource in demonology and exorcisms. Here I am going to give you some examples of the evaluation process. These can sometimes be a painstaking process as you have to not only consider the client but the client's family history. Someone can have no indication of a mental disorder, but if it is in their family history, we must take that into account. Some mental illnesses can be caused by triggers such as physical traumas, stress, and diet.

I'm sure it sounds as though there is a lot of stuff to get to before we take on the big bad, but that is because there is. It is so important to be absolutely sure and rule out all of the other causes before attempting an exorcism that wouldn't work because the healing needed for the mind cannot occur. The evaluations are not just written on paper; for some of the phenomena, we must look at the environment, check the pipes for banging, the chimney for howling, the door and floorboards for creaking etc.. Usually, if we can prove that it is a mundane cause, it makes the client feel so much better. However, there is not always a physical answer, and that is what this important step is for. Here are some examples of questions I ask, use them as you will, to make your own evaluation forms.

QUESTIONNAIRE

What have you been experiencing?
(Ask the client to list dates and times to the best of their memory—this could later prove important.)

Are you the only person in the home or family that has had experiences?
(It is important if they say there are others that you interview them.)

Have you ever been treated for a mental disorder?
(Such as depression, bi-polar, schizophrenia, DID—aka Multiple Personality Disorder.)

What is the earliest memory of your life?
(People with multiple personality disorder can only usually remember from ages 6-11; usually soon after they begin to have black-out periods of some sort.)

Are you currently on any prescribed or over-the-counter medications?
(Remember, even some over the counter medicines may have hallucinatory side effects if not taken responsibly.)

Have you taken any of these medications in the last 72 hours?
(Medicines taken regularly usually stay in the system long after the patient is finished taking them, typically 48-72 hours, sometimes longer depending on how long they have been on the medication.)

What is your current ideology, belief system, or religion?
(This can impact any potential exorcism enormously, because you want to have your methods correspond as much as possible with the belief system of the victim. It will create a stronger impression on the victim and the entity.)

At what age did you start having experiences?

(A lot of victims will express that they have seen things from a very, very young age; typically this is unrelated to the believed demonic attack, however it can show their sensitivity to spirit phenomena and may prove vital within the investigation as many people confuse spirits with demons.)

Have you been noticing any arguments with the home, either between family members or friends who come to visit?

(This is common for all three types of entities, spirits, demonic, and negative thoughtform.)

Any sudden onsets of depression, melancholy, or suicidal thoughts? If yes, what were the circumstances around them?

(Sometimes demonic entities try to control their potential host bodies by creating sadness and depression, with a "Keep 'em down and keep kicking" attitude.)

Have you gone to any yard sales, flea markets, buy any antiques off the Internet? If so, what were the items and when did you purchase them?

(Yes it is true, both spirits, demonic entities, and thoughforms can be attached to items.)

Have you or anyone else in the house used a Ouija Board? If so, how long ago, how many times have you used it, and where is it commonly kept?

(Sometimes the activity is in direct correlation with where the Ouija Board is kept because the spirit wants to speak. It will make itself known in any way possible even if it may seem "evil.")

Have you or anyone else in the home bought any books on demons, old occult, summoning, or incantations? If so when, were they ever used, where are they now?

(This question is very important, due to the fact that a lot of these books only have the summoning part and if they were in fact used, it would make it a lot easier for the occultist to banish the entity.)

Do you experience any phenomena right before going to sleep or right when you wake up? Seeing people or forms, bed or yourself vibrating, feeling paralyzed, dizzy and out of sorts?

(There are a couple of reasons this could be happening apart from spirit or demonic attack. Firstly, there was a study done which concluded that sometimes our dreams and reality blend a little when we first awaken or begin to fall asleep, so it may induce hallucinations. The other part is considered OBE, also known as astral travel or out of body experience. When we fall asleep, often we have dreams of flying or visiting friends and family; sometimes these dreams are so strong, we would believe it happened. Well, it most likely did. When we dream, it gives the soul free reign to leave the body and wander. However, if we wake up too quickly, sometimes it can feel as though you are hitting cement, the bed will literally bounce as if you have fallen, it can feel as though you or the bed is vibrating as your soul's energy and body's energy realign, or you can feel paralyzed and your body does not respond— this is due to the fact that your soul is not completely back in the body yet. A lot of people have experienced this phenomena and attributed it to spirits, poltergeists, or demons when it was in fact their own spirit causing the problem.)

These are some of the most important questions I ask and they are very good for anyone to ask a client as they look to identify a potential spirit or demonic. It is important that, no matter what, all bases are covered. Most likely, if you have picked up this book, then you have had a previous interest in demonology and exorcism. It is imperative as you continue on your journey to think of new questions to ask clients and keep updated on information concerning the field. Remember to try and phrase your questions in an open-ended way. If the victim is indeed being attacked, you know the signs and they will tell you. There are always new theories and ideas being put out there, not just about demonology, but the paranormal in general. Be observant and keep an open mind.

THE TOOLS

 ools are very important. They are symbols the inhuman entities recognize and often fear. If you show a cross to a Catholic or Christian demonic entity, they will recognize it for the symbol it represents, not the two pieces of wood it took to make it. However, if you show that same cross to a hungry spirit or Ashipu, it wouldn't recognize the symbol. It is very important to know the idols and relics of many faiths so that, no matter what happens, an individual is always ready and prepared.

Here are some items every demonologist and exorcist needs on hand. You will come across many items along the way that are not listed here. Be careful when you first gather a tool—make sure to cleanse the item properly unless previously blessed by clergy. This is a simple thing to do; you can easily get a herb called White Sage, burn the herb, and run the tool through it. You can also place the item in sea salt (with no water) over night, or set it for a full cycle of the moon on a window sill where it will catch both the sun's rays and the moon's glow, this is imperative as many of the items you will collect will have had previous users or may have been manufactured. In any case, unless the item is already blessed, you would want to do so yourself.

THE HOLY CRUCIFIX

This is either made out of some type of wood or metal and formed into a cross, which represents the sacrifice that Jesus made for all mankind's sins. Some crosses are just the form of a cross, while others show Jesus nailed to the cross. The first recorded use of the crucifix was around the second century and used as a talisman against all powers of evil and demons.

PRAYER BOOKS

There seems to be a large number of prayer or exorcism books in the world, but we will cover the most popular ones used to banish evil and/or demons. The best known and most common source for exorcisms prayers is the *Rituale Romanum*, one of the official books of the Roman Rite. In 1586, Cardinal Giulio Antonio Santorio, of St. Severina, printed a handbook for priests, giving various popular rituals of the time. This book was the foundation for the Roman Ritual which Paul V said, *"He (Cardinal Santorio) had composed after long study with much industry and labor."*

In 1614, Paul V took this book and created an official first edition of the Roman Rite; this text was made up of "books" including the Breviary which dictates the laws and regulations of Mass, and canonical office, the Missal, which contains prayers that are used at the altar, chants, or songs that are used throughout the ecclesiastical year. There are ten chapters in the *Rituale Romanum,* including prayers, blessings, and of course, exorcism.

This holy book gained popularity in 1973, when it was used in the movie *The Exorcist;* this book is actually not the one and only of its kind—there are many different texts that give instruction on exorcism. Many countries blend their old pagan beliefs with that of the Church, causing different types of exorcism ceremonies to be practiced all over the world.

In fact, the Church of Milan has its own book called the *Ambrosian Liturgy and Rite*, named after St. Ambrose, the Bishop of Milan. Although there is no definitive proof that he wrote it, he has been talked about in connection with the text since the eighth century. This book is believed to have been written in the fourth century and includes its own version of exorcism.

The *Book Of Needs* is a very interesting text, if one can get their hands on; it is now known as the *Orthodox Book of Prayers*, but was also known as the *Great Euchologion*. It was mainly compiled by St. Basil and St. John Chrysostom and included three prayers of exorcism by St. Basil and four from St. Chrysostom including prayers on releasing demons from animals. It has much more than exorcisms, though, and includes prayers for sickness, protection, Divine Liturgies and more.

The *Bon-Po Books of the Dead* were based on a religion that developed at the same time as Tibetan Buddhism. During the time, Bon-Po practitioners believed their lives were connected to that of their leader or king. Since they saw their King as a god figure, they created elaborate ceremonies and rituals to bring good health to him, extend his life, and protect him. When the King ultimately died, they then had rituals which would ensure safe passage to the Other side. Bon (which is the name for the religion itself) has melded with Buddhism and other Tibetan belief systems to create what is now known distinctly as Tibetan Buddhism. There are no real exorcism texts within Buddhism, but there are in Bon-po. If you read *The Death Rituals of Tibetan Bon-Po's* and *Bon-Po Funeral Rites Eliminating All Evil Rebirths*, it discusses in detail pre-funerary rites, including exorcism of evil spirits to prevent a reanimation of the corpse.

HOLY WATER

Water often symbolizes spiritual cleansing. You can't talk about an aspergillum without discussing holy water. Before the modernization of holy water, it was usually a purified water with salt (blessed by a cleric) mixed in. Since the 1960s the Church has gotten rid of the salt, and has had priests simply bless the water itself. Although it doesn't seem to really matter which way the water is made, it is the blessing, that makes the water holy. Since the fifth century, Christians have used Holy Water, possibly even before then. They often used rivers to baptize new converts and children, which is in fact the oldest Christian practice known, before the Churches began to take the ceremony in doors.

This mystical liquid is not just a Catholic or Christian belief; many different cultures use some form of Blessed Water. The ancient Greek's holy water is called "chernips," and was made using a bucket of water and extinguishing a torch from a religious shrine in it. Muslims collect water from the Wall of ZamZam and use it in their holy blessings. Amrit, what the Sikhs call their holy water, mainly used it in the baptism ceremony. The ritual involves the drinking of the water which is created with different soluble materials, and then mixes with a Khanda (ritual knife); the Amrit is made while another person recites the five sacred Banis or chants. Hindu's use water from the Ganges, and Buddhist actually fill a new pot with water and keep it near them while performing the Paritrana Ceremony, which in itself blesses the water. The biggest ingredient in the creation of holy water is faith.

ASPERGILLUM

This tool is most commonly used in Anglican and Roman Catholic ceremonies and rituals. Typically, it is either a brush or short-handled tool with a perforated ball at the end. There is a sponge hidden inside which is soaked in the Holy Water so when shaken it, sprays the blessed water around. If you cannot afford to buy an aspergillum, your fingers will work just as well.

THE BOOK

It is important for you to always have a journal at your disposal to either take notes during a particular case or write down research that may be useful in the future. I keep my personal journal filled with prayers, exorcism rites, incantations, and magical symbols and seals that I use most often or have found to be more of an influence over demonic or evil spirits. It is also a wonderful way to see yourself grow as a demonologist, because you will end up with many journals detailing your road toward full knowledge of inhuman entities.

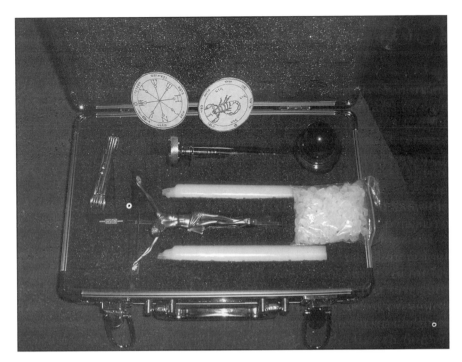

An example of some of Katie's favorite tools.

PHURBA

A Phurba is a three-sided and three-faced stake-like ritual tool used in Tibetan Buddhism or Bon. This instrument can be used to hold inhuman entities or negative thoughtforms in place after they have been disconnected from their host bodies. It can also be used to bind the energies and give purification to a person, place, or thing. The Phurba can be made of either metal or wood and is often consecrated by striking the dagger into the ground, or a basket or bowl of rice. The wooden Phurba is more commonly used for shamanic healing, and usually depicts two snakes or dragons also known as nāgas.

SHOFAR

The Shofar is a ram's horn that is used throughout the Jewish calendar. It is said that the Rabbi uses the horn in a certain way, hitting certain notes, so that the soul who is affecting the body would be "shaken" loose of its host. Where Catholic exorcism seeks to drive the demon away from the body and person, the Rabbi seeks to heal both human and spirit. After using the shofar to detach the dybbuk (see Chapter: Evil is in Every Culture) from the host body, the cleric usually begins to communicate with the entity, ask what it needs to move on, and then prays for the spirit.

OBSIDIAN (CRYSTAL)

This crystal is formed from magma; it is more of a glass than a crystal and is sometimes used in cardiac surgery because a well-cut obsidian blade is three times sharper than a steel surgical scalpel. Aside from that, Obsidian is great for when you are working a case that is not necessarily demonic. It absorbs negativity and breaks any evil influences that may be in or around the home or latched on to a person. You can find them easily and they are not that expensive depending on the type you buy.

There are many different varieties of obsidian, such as snowflake obsidian, metallic obsidian, and others. However, what you need is the purest obsidian you can find. I always keep three small obsidian balls in my case, just for the purpose of helping to rid the person or home of any negative energies in their environment. But what you need to be aware of is that while obsidian does keep hold of negative energy, it will also project your own negativity back to you, if you hold the ball for too long or gaze for long periods into it. Always keep it covered and in a dark place.

Now, I use my obsidians repeatedly and they do get full; you will know this because the crystal will actually begin to feel like a weight. When this happens, bury it. Leave it there for seven days and nights, then come back and dig it up. Your crystal will have released the energies back into the earth to be cleansed (the earth will use energy, either negative or positive, it does not matter, the fuel itself it has no negative repercussions on the environment or the habitants of the area) and will feel light again. This is how you know it is ready to go back to work.

Katie's Journal.

Prayers Of Exorcism and Protection

ere I present to you, from the four most recognized religions, prayers of both protection and exorcism. Some are written in their native tongue, others you will recognize as familiar, but each is special. You must remember everything you have learned within this book—faith and intent are the most powerful tools in your arsenal. There is a line from the bible that emphasizes this point.

> *"Do you believe that God is one? You do well!*
> *The demons also believe and tremble with fear!"*
>
> ~James 2:19

One must believe 100 percent in what they are doing; *know* it will work. The tiniest doubt will give the entity something to work with to break you down. I do not advocate attempting to use these prayers during an exorcism unless guided by someone with experience in the matter; do not attempt to conduct your own exorcism unless instructed by an authority in this field. You have weapons now, and that is a wonderful thing, but you must know when to retreat and when to fight. Choose wisely and be careful.

Catholic Protection Prayers

Our Father

> *Our Father, who art in heaven*
> *hallowed be thy Name,*
> *thy kingdom come,*
> *thy will be done,*
> *on earth as it is in heaven.*
> *Give us this day our daily bread*
> *And forgive us our trespasses,*
> *as we forgive those*
> *who trespass against us.*
> *And lead us not into temptation,*

but deliver us from evil.
For thine is the kingdom,
and the power, and the glory,
for ever and ever.
Amen.

Prayer to St. Anthony for Protection Against Danger

O Holy St. Anthony, be our protector and defender.
Ask God to surround us with the Holy Angels,
so that we may emerge from every danger
in the fullness of health and well being.
Guide our life journey,
so we will always walk safely together with you,
* in God's friendship.*
Amen

CATHOLIC PRAYERS OF EXORCISM

Prayer to Saint Michael
~Taken from the Roman Ritual

Most Glorious Prince of the Heavenly Armies, Saint Michael the Archangel defend us in "our battle against principalities and powers, against the rulers of this world of darkness, against the spirits of wickedness in the high places."

Come to the assistance of men whom God has created to His likeness, and whom He has redeemed at a great price from the tyranny of the Devil. Holy Church venerates thee as a great guardian and protector; to thee the Lord has entrusted the souls of the redeemed to be led into Heaven.

Pray therefore the God of Peace to crush Satan beneath our feet, that He may no longer retain men captive and do injury to the Church. Offer our prayers to the Most High, that without delay they may draw His mercy down upon us; "Take hold of the Dragon, the old Serpent, which is the Devil and Satan bind him and cast him into the bottomless pit so that he may no longer seduce the nations."

Catholic Prayer of Exorcism
~Taken From The Sacrament of Baptism of the Manual
of Prayers Archbishop of Baltimore 1889

Original: *Exorcizo te, omnis spiritus immunde, in nomine Dei Patris omnipotentis, et in noimine Jesu Christi Filii ejus, Domini et Judicis nostri, et in virtute Spiritus Sancti, ut descedas ab hoc plasmate Dei, quod Dominus noster ad templum sanctum suum vocare dignatus est, ut fiat templum Dei vivi, et Spiritus Sanctus habitet in eo. Per eumdem Christum Dominum nostrum, qui venturus est judicare vivos et mortuos, et saeculum per ignem.*

Translation: *I exorcise thee, unclean spirit in the name of God the Father Almighty, Jesus Christ, His only begotten Son and in the power of the Holy Spirit, that thou depart from this creature of God, which our Lord hath designed to unto His holy temple.*

I cast out you noxious vermin, through the same Christ our Lord, who shall come to judge the living and the dead, and the world by fire.

MUSLIM PROTECTION PRAYERS

English Translation of interpretation of meaning Quran 114 :1-6

Proclaim (O dear Prophet Mohammed – peace and blessings be upon him), "I take refuge of the One Who is the Lord of all mankind. The King of all mankind. The God of all mankind. From the evil of the one who instills evil thoughts in the hearts—and stays hidden. Those who instill evil thoughts into the hearts of men. Among the jinns and men."

Original: *Bismillahi alladhi la yadurru ma `a ismihi shay'un fi al-ardi wa la fi as-sama'i wa huwa as-sami `u al-`alim*

Translation: *In the name of Allah; with His name, nothing whatsoever on earth or heaven can inflict any harm; He is All-Hearing and All-Knowing*

Original: *Hasbiya Allahu la ilaha illa huwa `alayhi tawakkaltu wahuwa rabbu al-`arshi al-`azhim*

Translation: *Allah suffices me; there is no god but He; in Him I place my sole trust; He is the Lord of the mighty Throne.*

Original: *Allaahumma ini a`duhu bika min hamazati ash-shayatin wa a `udhu bika rabbi an yahdurun*

Translation: *O Allah, I seek refuge in You from the whisperings of Satan; my Lord, I seek refuge in You from their presence around me).*

Original: *A`udhu bi `izzati Allahi wa qudratihi mimma ajidu wa uhadhiru.*

Translation: *I seek refuge in Allah's glory and power from the affliction and pain I experience and suffer from.*

MUSLIM EXORCISM PRAYERS

"Bismillaahi arqeeka min kulli shay'in yu'dheeka, min sharri kulli nafsin aw 'aynin haasidin. Allaahu yashfeeka. Bismillaahi arqeek."

English Translation: *"In the name of Allaah I exorcise you from everything which harms you, from the evil of every soul or jealous eye. May Allaah cure you. In the name of Allaah I exorcise you."*

HINDU PRAYERS OF PROTECTION

Meditation On Lord Shiva

Original: *Shaantam padmaasanastham shashadharamakutam panchavaktram trinetram, Shoolam vajram cha khadgam parashumabhayadam dakshinaange vahantam; Naagam paasham cha ghantaam damaruka sahitam chaankusham vaamabhaage, Naanaalankaara deeptam sphatika maninibham paarvateesham namaami.*

Translation: *I prostrate myself before the five-faced Lord of Parvati, who is adorned with various ornaments, who shines like the crystal jewel, who is seated peacefully in the lotus pose, with moon-crested crown, with three eyes, wearing trident, thunderbolt, sword and axe on the right side, who holds the serpent, noose, bell, damaru and spear on the left side, and who gives protection from all fear to His devotees.*

The Gayatri Mantra

~ Taken from the Vedas

Oh God! Thou art the Giver of Life, Remover of pain and sorrow, The Bestower of happiness, Oh! Creator of the Universe, May we receive thy supreme sin-destroying light, May Thou guide our intellect in the right direction.

A U M   B H O O R   B H U W A H   S W A H A ,
T A T   S A V I T U R   V A R E N Y A M
B H A R G O   D E V A S A Y A   D H E E M A H I
DHIYO YO NAHA PRACHODAYAT

A Prayer and Charm Against Demons

~From Artharveda Book One

May Potent Agni who destroys the demons bless and shelter us.
From greedy fiends who rise at night-time when the moon is dark
Varuna's benison hath blessed this lead, and Agni strengthens it.
Indra hath given me the lead: this verily repels the fiends.
This overcomes Vishkandha - this drives the voracious fiends away:
By means of this have I o'erthrown all the Pisachi's demon brood.
If thou destroy a cow of ours, a human being, or a steed
We pierce thee with this peace of lead
So that thou mayst not slay our men.

HINDU PRAYERS OF EXORCISM

Excerpt 1 From A Prayer for the Destruction of Demons

~From Artharvaveda Book Eight

O Jatavedas, armed with teeth of iron, enkindled with thy flame, attack the demons.
Seize with thy tongue the foolish gods' adorers:
rend, put within thy mouth the raw-flesh-eaters.
Apply thy teeth, the upper and the lower, thou who hast both, enkindled and destroying.
Roam also in the air, O King, around us, and with thy jaws assail the wicked spirits.
Pierce through the Yatudhana's skin,
O Agni; let the destroying
dart with fire consume him.

Rend his joints, Jatavedas!
Let the eater of raw flesh, seeking flesh, tear and destroy him.
Where now thou seest, Agni Jatavedas!
A Yatudhana, standing still or roaming.
Or one that flieth through the air's mid-region, kindled to fury
as an archer pierce him.
Bending thy shafts through sacrifices,
Agni! Dipping thine arrows in the hymn to point them,
Pierce to the heart therewith the Yatudhanas, and break
Their arms uplifted to attack thee.
Rescue the captives also, Jatavedas! yea, those whom
Yatudhanas' spears have captured.
Strike down that fiend, blazing before him, Agni!
Let spotted carrion-eating kites devour him.

Excerpt 2 From A Prayer for the Destruction of Demons
~From Artharvaveda Book Eight

Agni! thee, a sage,
In conquering colour day by day, destroyer of the treacherous foe.
With deadly poison strike thou back the treacherous brood of
Rakshasas,
O Agni, with thy sharpened glow, with rays that flash with
points of flame.
Agni shines far and wide with lofty splendour, and by
his great-ness makes all things apparent.
He conquers godless and malign enchantments, and sharpens
both his horns to gore the ogres.
Thy two unwasting horns, O Jatavedas, keen-pointed
weapons, sharpened by devotion
With these transfix the wicked-souled Kimidin, with fierce flame,
Jatavedas! when he meets thee
Bright, radiant, meet to be adored, immortal with
Refulgent, glow, Agni drives Rakshasas away.

A Prayer to Agni For the Destruction Of Evil Spirits
~From Artharvaveda Book One

God Agni hath come forth to us, fiend-slayer, chaser of disease,
Burning the Yatudhanas up, Kimidins, and deceitful ones.
Consume the Yatudhanas, God! meet the Kimidins
with thy flame:
Burn up the Yatudhanis as they face thee,
thou whose path is black!

She who hath cursed us with a curse, or hath conceived a
  murderous sin;
Or seized our son to take his blood, let her devour the child she bare.
Let her, the Yatudhani eat son, sister, and her daughter's child.
Now let the twain by turns destroy the wild-haired Yatudhanis-
and crush down Arayis to the earth!

JEWISH PRAYERS OF PROTECTION

Prayer for Protection
~Taken from the Babylonian Talmud

O Lord, grant that this night we may sleep in peace.
And that in the morning our awakening may also be in peace.
May our daytime be cloaked in your peace.
Protect us and inspire us to think and act only out of love.
Keep far from us all evil;
May our paths be free from all obstacles from when we go until
we return home.

Psalm of Protection
~Taken from Psalms 27: 1-3, Tanakh (Jewish Publication Society 1917)

HaShem is my light and my salvation; whom shall I fear?
HaShem is the stronghold of my life; of whom shall I be afraid?
When evil-doers came upon me to eat up my flesh,
Even mine adversaries and my foes, they stumbled and fell.
Though a host should encamp against me, my heart shall not fear;
Though war should rise up against me, even then will I be confident.

JEWISH PRAYERS OF EXORCISM

There aren't any real "prayers" to rid oneself of the dybbuk; however, there are rituals. Here I will show you an excerpt from the *Shashon Yesod ha-Olam* a medieval Hebrew magical manual; it details the exorcism of a dybbuk. But I am just going to give an example of one of the adjurations.

"I adjure you, the pure and holy angels Michael, Gabriel, Shuviel,
Ahadriel, Zumtiel, Yechutriel, Zumtziel...by 72 names I adjure you,

you all the retinues of spirits in the world—Be'ail Lachush and all your retinue; Kapkafuni the Queen of Demons and all your retinue; and Agrat bat Malkat and all your retinue, and Zmamit and all your retinue, and those that were made on the eve of the Shabbat that you bring forth that demon immediately and do not detain the mazzik of so-and-so, and tell me his name in this circle that I have drawn in your honor...Immediately they will tell you his name and the name of the father and the name of his mother aloud; do not fear.

~ Translated by Jeffrey Chajes an Israeli Scholar

Don't be a Loner

Working with Paranormal Groups

worked as a demonologist for a very long time on my own, and while I helped many people, it was a blessing when I met Beckah (Tolley) Boyd and Raven Duclos which whom later we formed Ghost Quest, a paranormal research society. They accepted my unique way of dealing with demonic entities through the occult. True demonologists are a rare breed; many do not have the capacity to do exorcisms on their own and reach out to a church or higher authority. As you now know, I do not send my findings to the church for review. Working with a paranormal group is a great experience, and one that I encourage all budding demonologists to try. Many of us start working on our own and inevitably join a group—and there are many advantages to having a team of support when you are facing the demonic entity.

All paranormal groups operate differently; like ours, we have two psychics, myself the demonologist, and a locations manager. Others have maybe have six to thirty people who are just investigators or hold a specific role within the group—either way, they all have a common goal. They are there to help the afflicted, again though done in different way. In my group, we mix science and spirituality, creating a unique blend of evidence and bringing help to both victim and spirit. Others bring help to the client through evidence alone, just by proving something is there sometimes can relieve a victim's anxiety about the situation.

Whichever way you lean towards, please be aware that there are a few simple questions you can ask the lead investigator and a few easy-to-find things you should see on their web sites (listed later in the chapter). But for those of you looking to start your own group, here are a few things to keep in mind.

If you plan to start your own group, we suggest joining a more experienced research society before venturing out on your own, as fieldwork is the best way to gain experience, and joining another group for however long is the greatest way to do it safely.

Most will never get rich doing paranormal research; it is a labor of love, not a way to fame. Some groups will charge dues to cover fees for travel, supplies, and equipment. Some groups specialize in certain areas of research like business properties or homes; others are up for anything. When looking into a paranormal group, there are many things to take into account, you want a group that has been around the block a couple of times and has a good reputation. Some groups are just starting out, but that doesn't mean they don't know what they are doing. It is important to find out from the lead investigator if they were a part of another group and if so, how long. You want to know that your safety will be ensured to the best ability of the group.

It is important to know there are some groups who claim to have experience, but in fact don't. There are some who do not act with respect towards the field. These issues need to be discussed before making any type of commitment. There are several different ways to gather evidence, and some groups rate one method over another— like they would prefer pictorial evidence to electronic voice phenomena; then there are some who will look at the whole.

Oftentimes, groups will put you through a probationary period to test the waters with a new member. This gives you the opportunity to look at how they work and figure out if it is something you really want to do. If they do not have a probationary period, be sure that if you have to fill out a form, you read it carefully—some have a no-compete clause and this will not allow you to join another group if you decide you didn't care for the team.

When looking for a group, you will find the most information in a face-to-face meeting with the lead investigator or investigators where you can read body language, and hear their honest responses.

Here are the questions and key words to look for when talking with a lead investigator or researching web sites.

Ghost Quest crew.

QUESTIONNAIRE
FOR PARANORMAL GROUPS

1. How long has the paranormal group been investigating or operating?

2. How many members are in the paranormal group?

3. How does the group approach the investigations, scientifically or spiritually?

4. How long is an apprenticeship?

5. Do you have a membership fee or dues program?

6. What equipment does the group use?

7. What does the group look for in an investigator?

8. Is the group a member of any other paranormal investigative network?

9. What type of evidence do you feel is the most convincing or important?

10. Does the group have psychics, demonologists, or spiritual advisors?

11. What type of places does the group investigate the most? Homes, businesses, cemeteries?

12. What is the time commitment the group expects from me?

13. Do you have a uniform or other ways of identifying the team while on site or at public events?

When researching web sites, you want to be able to view the pictorial evidence if it is available. There are many new groups (and some older ones) who may not necessarily know how to collect hard evidence. I have seen many pictures of "ectoplasm" that was in fact cigarette smoke. Many so badly want to prove the existence of the supernatural, they will convince themselves that something is evidence when it is not. Be aware of this; also be on the lookout for any disrespectful behavior on the web site or in the evidence, such as drinking while on investigations, or middle-finger photos. Look at their case files if available. Do they protect the identity of the victims or clients? I have heard more than once about a paranormal group giving away information that they were asked not to. Look for connections with other groups of a larger nature, either a part of the same group or an affiliate. Check out the larger group's site; if it is an affiliation, then more than likely, the group was trained or partially taught by the larger group. You would get a better idea of how they work from the original group's site. You want to check out any promotional areas they are doing such as radio shows, newspaper articles, books, television appearances, and so forth. If they have done any promotion, then watch, listen, or read what has been said or covered about them. This could be an important part of making your decision depending on whether you agree with what you hear, see, or read.

CONCLUSION

emonology is an ever growing field, with new experiences, researchers, and ideas popping up all the time. Whether you see demons as many modern occultists do—that it is just our shadow selves, the inherent polarity to our goodness, or something outside of ourselves threatening and inherently evil—either way, you now have the tools to begin your journey into the realm of demons.

I am sure psychology and sciences will continue to attempt to explain away many of the factors that are attributed to demonic possession and hauntings. Because of that, demonologists, exorcists, and clergy must remain on their toes to keep up with the ever-changing attitudes towards these entities. You are now equipped with the information necessary to discover whether or not there are demons in a home, and the different entities that share this world with us—however, this book is just the tip of the iceberg. There are thousands of beings that are unseen to the naked eye, that both help and hinder us, protect and attack us. As the world continues to open itself to the spiritual realms, we must learn to accept all forms of creatures we may encounter.

This book does not make you into an automatic demonologist, exorcist, or occultist; this is not a certification program. This is a guide and a beginning for you. Tread carefully.

As you delve deeper into the world of demons and the paranormal, there are three things to remember:

1. Be prepared.
2. Be aware.
3. And be careful.

IN SPIRIT,

KATIE BOYD

RESOURCES

Katie Boyd's Websites:
www.ancientwisdomnh.com (Katie's official web page)
www.ghostquest.org (NH's leading paranormal research society.)

Psychics Resources:
(Katie also works with a certain psychic on private cases.)
Beckah Boyd Psychic Consultations; www.ancientwisdomnh.com/Beckah.htm

Demonology Resources:
http://www.muttaqun.com (to learn about Islamic Faith and the Jinni.)

Exorcism
http://www.answers.com/topic/exorcism (discusses the history and folklore surrounding exorcism.)
www.whatstheharm.net/exorcisms.htm (Information and list about death by exorcism.)
www.unsolvedmysteries.com/usm81745.html (A list of exorcism fatalities.)

Psychology Resources:
www.wrongdiagnosis.com (awesome web site we use for gathering the list of medications with hallucination side effects.)
www.schizophrenia.com/diag.php (great resource for study of schizophrenia.)

Occult Resources:
(Here are some sites which cover sacred texts, magical formulas, and more.)
www.sacred-texts.com
www.esotericarchives.com/solomon/lemegeton.htm
www.sacred-magick.com
www.darkart.homestead.com/grimoires.html
www.controverscial.com
www.jewishencyclopedia.com
www.crystalworlds.com/Crystals_Meanings.htm
www.themystica.org/mystica/articles/t/tetragrammatiom.html

Language Translators:
www.translation-guide.com
www.stars21.com/translator
www.lexicool.com

Alchemy Resources:
www.levity.com
www.spagyria.com
www.crucible.org/modern_alchemy.htm
www.alchemylab.com

Paranormal Talk Radio Sites:
(These are a great resource to the paranormal world.)

C.J. EVP Research Talk Radio
www.hauntingsradio.com
www.ghostlytalk.com
www.ccspookcentral.com
www.cprshow.com
Shadowsinthedarkradio.com
Hot Paratalk Radio
Haunted Survivor Radio
www.para-xradio.com
Stiring The Cauldron Talk Radio
Ghost Chatter Talk Radio
Ghostology Talk Radio
Parahub Talk Radio

Paranormal Resource Web sites:
GhostQuest.org
Planetparanormal.com
Strangeusa.com
Skepdic.com
Williamflud.com
Theshadowlands.net
Haunted-places.com

INDEX

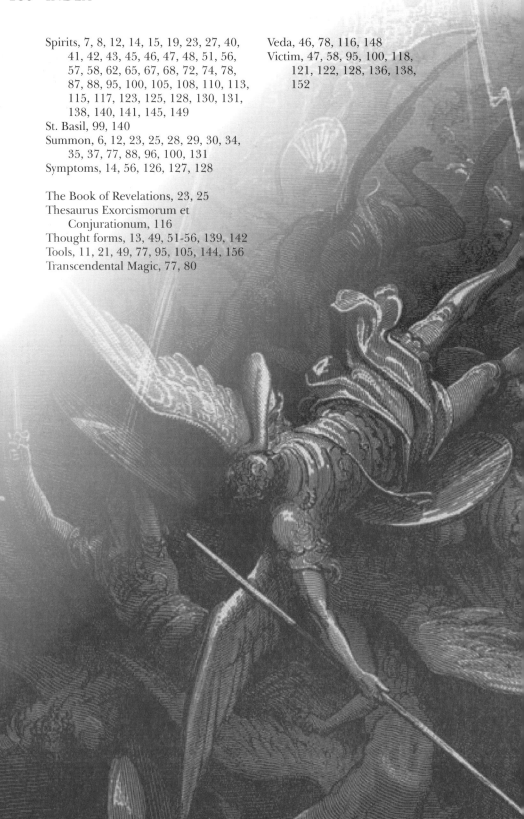